@Copyright 2019by Blanca Tull- **All rights reserved.**

This document is geared towards providing exact and reliable information in regards to the topic and issue covered. The publication is sold with the idea that the publisher is not required to render accounting, officially permitted, or otherwise, qualified services. If advice is necessary, legal or professional, a practiced individual in the profession should be ordered.

Under no circumstance will any legal responsibility or blame be held against the publisher for any reparation, damages, or monetary loss due to the information herein, either directly or indirectly.

Legal Notice: The book is copyright protected. This is only for personal use. You cannot amend, distribute, sell, use, quote or paraphrase any part or the content within this book without the consent of the author.

Disclaimer Notice: Please note the information contained within this document is for educational and entertainment purposes only. Every attempt has been made to provide accurate, up to date and reliable complete information. No warranties of any kind are expressed or implied. Readers acknowledge that the author is not engaging in the rendering of legal, financial, medical or professional advice. The content of this book has been derived from various sources. Please consult a licensed professional before attempting any techniques outlined in this book.

CONTENTS

Ketogenic Diet..6

Benefits of Keto Diet..17

Health issues regarding Ketogenic Diets...19

What are the main benefits and how you can maximize them?............21

Additional Advantages...24

Tips and Tricks for Making A Keto Lifestyle Easier..................................25

Why 21 Days Meal Plan?...29

My Experience with Diet...33

Vegetables and Side Dishes Recipes..34

    Broccoli Cheese Soup...34

    Mediterranean Spinach with Cheese..35

    Cheesy Cauliflower..36

    Parmesan Roasted Bamboo Sprouts..37

    Mexican Cheesy Veggies..38

    Green Beans with Mushrooms and Bacons...39

    Cauliflower Mash...40

    Bacon Wrapped Asparagus...41

    Cheesy Brussels Sprout..42

    Tomato Soup..43

Poultry Recipes...44

    Creamy Chicken Thighs...44

    Ham Stuffed Turkey Rolls...45

    Cheesy Chicken Tenders..46

Chili Lime Turkey... 47

Stuffed Whole Chicken.. 48

Mediterranean Turkey Cutlets... 49

Caprese Hasselback Chicken.. 50

Keto Garlic Turkey Breasts.. 51

Air Fried Chicken... 52

Creamy Turkey Breast... 53

Beef Recipes.. 54

Garlic Creamy Beef Steak... 54

Ketogenic Beef Sirloin Steak... 55

Beef Fajitas.. 56

Mexican Taco Casserole... 57

Beef Roast... 58

Keto Minced Meat.. 59

Beef Curry.. 60

Grilled Beef Steak.. 61

2-Meat Chili.. 62

Keto Low Carb Meat Balls... 63

Pork Recipes... 64

Jamaican Jerk Pork Roast... 64

Bacon Swiss Pork Chops.. 65

Pork Carnitas... 66

Mustard Pork Chops.. 67

Zesty Pork Chops.. 68

Greek Pork Gyros.. 69

Crispy Parmesan Crusted Pork Chops... 70

Roasted Pork 71

Fabulous Grilled Pork 72

Dinner Pork Tenderloin 73

Fish and Seafood Recipes 74

Mahi Mahi Cakes 74

Salmon Stew 75

Paprika Shrimp 76

Ketogenic Butter Fish 77

Shrimp Magic 78

Omega-Rich Dinner 79

Sweet and Sour Fish 80

Buttered Scallops 81

Buffalo Fish 82

BBQ Trout 83

Eggs and Dairy Recipes 84

Scrambled Eggs 84

Pepperoni Omelet 85

Eggs Stuffed with Avocado and Watercress 86

Cheesy Mini Frittatas 87

Keto Coconut Pancakes 88

Nut Porridge 90

Lemon Mousse 91

Vanilla Yogurt 92

Low Carb Blueberry Muffins 93

Keto Quiche 94

Vegetarian Recipes 95

Tofu with Mushrooms..95

Bacon Veggies Combo..96

Onion Tofu Scramble..97

Ham Spinach Blast..98

Bacon Bok Choy Samba...99

Garlic Parmesan Fried Eggplant..100

Roasted Broccoli and Cauliflower...101

Creamed Peas..102

Whole Garlic Roast..103

Grilled Halloumi Salad..104

Snacks and Appetizers Recipes...105

Spinach Quiche..105

Cheese Casserole..106

Mixed Nuts...107

Broccoli Pops...108

Keto Onion Rings..109

Mexican Inspired Beef Soup..110

Zucchini Cream Cheese Fries..111

Asparagus Bites...112

Scallion Cake...113

Avocado Chips..114

Conclusion..115

Ketogenic Diet

What is ketogenic Diet?

The ketogenic diet has gained immense popularity due to its amazing health benefits. It works by cutting down the intake of carbohydrates and increasing the amount of the fat in the diet. Thus, the keto dietary approach allows the body to harness the extra energy through the breakdown of fats. It makes our body fat dependent while transforming it as less carb dependent. This change results in great health advantages like loss of body fat deposits, maintenance of blood sugar levels, etc. There are many other perks of switching to a keto diet. The word ketogenic is basically derived from ketosis, which is a metabolic process of breaking down fats in the absence of carbohydrates to produce energy and ketones. In the absence of sugars or carbs, the body stays free from harmful radicals and works more efficiently.

Switching to a Ketogenic Diet

Ketogenic is not simply a diet; it is a whole lifestyle that many consumers may misinterpret. Being a lifestyle means that you not only need some dietary changes to get to the perks of the ketosis, but you also need to turn your whole routine according to those changes. In sum, keto meals must accompany routine exercise, hydration, and proper sleep. A combination of all these changes will result in the keto-oriented health effects.

When a person switches to a ketogenic diet, he or she goes through three important phases:

1. Induction Phase:

When one enters the world of the ketogenic diet, it requires more mental strength than physical. It is important to prepare your mind for it and then act on it. Thus, the first phase is all about preparing yourself for this special diet. An easy way is by removing all the possible high carb food items from your groceries and opting for more clean carbs. Do your research and plan things out for yourself. Be steadier and more gradual to have a more lasting impact. Start limiting the number of carbs and keep track of the fat intake. Habit and discipline are most important while surviving this phase. Loss of will means loss of efforts, so start sticking to the routine!

2. Adjustment Phase:

Now that the induction phase has passed, the adjustment phase allows a person to add more variety to the diet using a variety of keto friendly fruits and vegetables. It is safe to integrate more fats to the diet through cream, cheeses or vegetable oils. In this phase, the body goes through slight changes in terms of energy levels and health. This adjustment in the diet is important to keep up with the pace of those changes.

3: Fitness Phase:

The last phase is the fitness phase. By this time, the routine for the keto diet must be well developed. However, the body still needs a kick start to burn more fat than glucose. A little exercise is recommended at this stage to help achieve the aim. Such exercise may range from light intensity aerobics to high-intensity exercises. Physical exercises, together with a planned ketogenic diet, are the road to a healthy and active life. The keto diet triggers the production of ketones inside the body. These ketone masses are then used as an energy source instead of glucose. The 'keto' part of the ketogenic diet plan is extracted from this. The ketones act as energy sources while the amount of sugar in the body is low.

Carbohydrate intake is inversely proportional to the production of the ketones in the body, meaning the less carb intake, the higher the ketones. Ketones are not directly produced through food breakdown; rather, the processing of fat results in the ketonic production. These ketones are essential for vital brain functions. This reason justifies why the first ketogenic diet was used only to cure patients of epilepsy and other brain-related diseases, so switching to a ketogenic diet quickly results in better mental health.

Carbohydrates may provide energy instantly, but that amount is fleeting. As a result, a sugary meal can make your energy levels drain within an hour or so, whereas a keto diet provides energy through fat processing and consumption, which is long-lasting and much higher than provided through the same amount of carbs.

When Is the Ketogenic Diet Right for You?

Being safe and healthy, the Ketogenic diet plan is now being followed by millions of users. It helps to prevent many diseases without the use of medications. It strengthens the body both mentally and physically. However, for every diet specific plan, it is important to always consult a physician before opting for it. Many people suffer from internal weaknesses or special health complications, which may render ketogenic diet more destruction than beneficial. These conditions include:

- People with type 1 diabetes or taking insulin medications. A ketogenic diet in such cases can cause ketoacidosis, which is quite harmful and even fatal.

- People with blood pressure complications should also ask a professional before opting for ketogenic lifestyle.

- Breastfeeding mothers.

Signs that you are on a ketogenic diet:

Many individuals ask about when the actual sign of ketosis appears? It reiterates that you are in the right direction and following the diet correctly. Since this diet benefits us more internally than externally for normal people, it is hard to witness the changes visually. There are however certain related signs which help us predict the direction correctly, and those hints are:

- **Dry Mouth and Constant Thirst:**

Right from the induction phase, ketosis can render more dehydration and requires more water intake than usual. In turn, when a person switches to the diet, it gives a constant feeling of thirst. Making your body fat dependent is a major shift, which can cause a temporary electrolyte imbalance as the body molds to adopt it. That is why try to drink as much water as possible on a daily basis.

- **Increased Urination:**

Acetoacetate is the compound which is a ketosis byproduct. It ends up in the urine and produces a constant urge of urination. Moreover, more water intake in the diet also adds to the frequent urination. These two reasons together can cause an increased rate of urination, which is a healthy sign as it allows the toxins to release out of the body more frequently.

- **Ketogenic breath:**

It is interesting to know for many that when we switch to a ketogenic diet, it also affects our breath and renders a smell fruitier like a nail polish remover. It is mainly because acetone is released from the body through the mouth. It happens of quite a few days after starting the ketogenic diet, but it disappears with time. The same smell can be sensed through the body sweat.

- **High Energy Level:**

The most visible sign of a keto diet is elevated levels of energy. The concentration level increases and a person can feel a spark in the body. Such positive energy can last throughout the day both physically and mentally.

- **Lower Need to Eat:**

This impact happens because the body has shifted from glucose to fats as energy sources. Keto followers are satisfied with eating once or twice a day, so it leads to unconscious intermittent fasting. This appetite suppression aids a lot in losing weight, is time efficient, and financially feasible.

What are the Perks of a Keto Diet?

The ketogenic diet has numerous advantages due to its selective approach. Every meal that we eat is an energy booster that is equally healthy. This secret fuels the popularity of the keto plan. It has outpaced all other dietary plans in the race due to its rich and healthy content. Let's explore more of its pros before switching to the plan.

1. Fat Burn

The main objective of a keto diet is to consume fats as a source of energy instead of carbohydrates. Therefore, when a person is on a keto diet, more fats present in the body are burnt, which consequently reduce weight and prevent obesity.

2. Lower Cholesterol:

Consumption of fats in the energy-producing process means decreased cholesterol levels in the blood. This change is particularly important for patients suffering from cardiovascular diseases and higher cholesterol levels.

3. Lower Blood Sugar:

Diabetes or high blood sugar level is caused due to zero or minimum production of insulin hormone in the body. People suffering from such disorder cannot regulate their blood sugar levels naturally; therefore, they need a diet low on sugars, and the ketogenic is one best options for such individuals.

4. Increased Energy:

A single fat molecule can produce three times more energy than a carbohydrate when broken down. This reason validates how the use of the ketogenic diet gives us an instant and long-lasting boost of energy after a meal.

5. Vitality:

Though scientists are still trying to cite direct evidence of the effects of ketogenic diet on the increased vitality of a person; however, they are convinced that keto food improves health in the longer run, foster an active metabolism, and detoxifies the body regularly, which all can lead to increased vitality.

6. Mental focus:

While it is true that the ketogenic diet was originally used for the treatment illnesses like epilepsy and Alzheimer, it is also true that lesser consumption of carbohydrates and more availability of ketones in the body detoxify the blood and nourished neural cells.

7. Reduce obesity:

There is a huge misconception that intake of more fats can cause obesity. It is true when that you accrue fats along with excessive carbohydrates. Yet fats in the keto diet do not cause obesity; instead, it reduces it by consuming all the deposited fats in the body.

8. Metabolism:

Increased energy production through ketosis leads to better metabolism. Due to the presence of fat molecules in the food, the bodywork rigorously works during and after the digestion to generate energy.

What to Eat on a Ketogenic Diet?

To make things simple and easier, let's break it down a little and try to understand the Keto diet plan. Kindly refer to the chart that explains what to have and what not to have. Below is a brief list of all items which can be used on a Ketogenic diet.

- **All Meats:**

All types of meat are free from carbohydrates, so it is always safe to use meat in the ketogenic diet. However, processed meat, which may contain high traces of carbohydrates, should be avoided.

- **Selective Vegetables:**

Keep in mind that not all vegetables are low on carbs. There are some who are full of starch, and they need to be avoided. A simple technique to access the suitability of the vegetables for a keto diet is to check if they are 'grown above the ground' or 'below it.' All vegetables grown underground are a no go for Keto, whereas vegetables which are grown above are best for keto and these mainly include cauliflower, broccoli, zucchini, etc. Among the vegetables, all the leafy green vegetables can be added to this diet, which include spinach, kale, parsley, cilantro, etc.

- **Dry Nuts and Seeds etc.:**

Nuts and seeds like sunflower seeds, pistachios, pumpkin seeds, almonds, etc. can all be used on a ketogenic diet.

- **Selective Dairy:**

Not every dairy product is allowed on a keto diet. For example, milk is prohibited for keto, whereas hard cheeses, high fat cream, butter, eggs, etc. can all be consumed.

- **Keto friendly Fruits:**

Not all berries are Keto friendly, so only choose blackberries or raspberries, and other low carb berries. Similarly, not all fruits can be taken on a keto diet. In essence, avocado, coconut, and others are keto friendly, but orange, apples, and pineapple, and others are high in carbohydrates.

- **All Fats:**

Ghee, butter, plant oils, animal fats all forms of fats can be used on a ketogenic diet.

- **Keto substitute:**

As sugar is strictly forbidden for a ketogenic diet, may it be brown or white there is a certain substitute which can be used like:

- Stevia
- Erythritol
- Swerve
- Monk fruit,
- Natvia
- Other low-carb sweeteners

What Should I Avoid on a Keto Diet?

Avoiding carbohydrates is the main aim of a ketogenic diet. Most of the daily items we use contain a high amount of carbohydrates in the form of sugars or starch. In fact, any amount of these items can drastically increase the carbohydrate value of your meal. So, it is best to avoid their use completely.

1. All Grains including Rice and Wheat:

All types of grains are high in carbohydrates, whether it's rice, corn, or wheat, as well as products extracted from them, as they are equally high in carbs, like corn flour, wheat flour or rice flour. So, while you need to avoid these grains for keto, their flours should also be averted. Coconut and almond flours can be used as a good substitute.

2. All Legumes including lentils and beans:

Legumes are also the underground parts of the plants; thus, they are highly rich in carbohydrates. Make no mistake of using them in your diet. These examples include all sorts of beans, from lima to chickpeas, garbanzo, black, white, red beans, etc. Be sure to cross all of them off your grocery list if you are about to go keto. All types of lentils are also banned on a keto diet.

3. Every Natural and Synthetic Sugar:

Besides white and brown sugar, there are other forms of it, which are also not keto friendly. This list includes honey, agave, molasses, maple syrup, etc. Also, avoid chocolates which are high in sugar. Use special sweeteners and sugar-free chocolates only.

4. High Carb Fruits:

Certain fruits need to be avoided while on a keto diet. Apples, bananas, oranges, pineapple, etc. all fall into that category. Do not use them in any form. Avoid using their flesh, juices, and pulp to keep your meal carb free.

5. Underground Tubers:

Tubers are basically underground vegetables, and some of them are rich in carbs including potatoes, yams, sweet potatoes, beets, etc.

6. Animal Milk:

As stated above, not all dairy products can be freely used on a ketogenic diet. Animal milk should be strictly avoided.

Benefits of Keto Diet

Body Shape:
Most people tend to go on this diet because it helps weight loss. Studies have shown that it is a faster method of weight reduction than traditional dieting approaches.

Cholesterol and Sugar Control:
It also helps to decrease cholesterol levels and type-2 diabetes. It has proven to be an effective method to control sugar.

Mental Capability:
Ketones tend to be a good source of fuel for the mind. Without carbohydrates, there are fewer chances of increments in sugar, which help concentration.

reduce seizures:
Many studies suggest how this diet can reduce seizures, especially in children. Keto can be done alongside minimal medications.

Controlling Blood Pressure:
It is known to help cholesterol and blood pressure, as it helps to improve triglyceride levels.

Help with Skin Problems:

A significant difference reduction in acne has been seen in people who try this diet. Excessive amounts of carbs can be a leading cause of skin problems. The ketogenic diet has helped this problem tremendously.

Health issues regarding Ketogenic Diets

There are a few complications regarding the intake of ketogenic diets. The most common encompass the following:

Cramps:

Cramps can be caused due to the lack of magnesium in the body. The most common cramp involves leg cramps, which often happen on the beginning of starting a ketogenic diet. This side effect usually happens in the mornings or nights and is the result of lacking minerals like magnesium in the body. Fluid intake and magnesium supplements help in overcoming this issue.

Constipation:

The main reason for constipation is lack of fluid or more commonly known as dehydration. It can be overcome by increasing fluid consumption to almost one gallon per day and with non-starchy vegetables with fibers.

Heart Palpitations

It is also common to note that while converting on a ketogenic diet, a person's heart rate is faster and harder than normal. Normally high fluid intake and sufficient salt consumption will overcome the problem: if it doesn't, then potassium supplements will help in overcoming the issue,

Effects on Physical Performance:
A person's physical performance may reduce while converting on a ketogenic diet. This impact is because the body is getting adjusted to using fat for the body needs. Once it gets adjusted, everything will be fine, as cycling carbs before a workout may help.

What are the main benefits and how you can maximize them?

There are numerous health benefits of the keto diet, which makes it different, more attractive, and promising than other low carb diet plans. The benefits of the keto diet deliver more powerful, effective, long-lasting results. A few prominent advantages of the keto diet plan are given as follows:

Lose Weight Drastically:
During the process of ketosis, the body changes its energy source from glucose to fat. When you switch to the keto diet, your body initially tends to consume your inner body fat for its working, logically explaining how effective it is in lowering down your weight. As soon as the insulin content in your body is dropped, fat loss is improved, and you lose weight without getting hungry. There are twenty studies that conclude that the keto diet is more efficient in weight loss than any other low carb diet plan.

Control Your Appetite:
The ketogenic diet is highly effective in controlling your appetite and hunger. The reason for this is that when the fats present in your body are burnt in a drastic manner, your body has access to them for its working without the need of having any external energy supply. You not only regulate your hunger with the keto diet but also help yourself in avoiding gaining weight, rather you lose weight. This appetite control assists in intermittent fasting, improves the conditions for reversing type-2 diabetes in addition to stimulating your weight loss. You can also save your hard earned money by not spending more on your takeout meals.

You can also refrain yourself from food and sugar addition apart from eating disorders like bulimia etc. by having a controlled appetite. This satisfaction of being full is the integral step of the solution. The keto plan makes your food your friend and an energy source, rather than your enemy.

Excessive Energy Levels and High Mental Performance:
During the process of ketosis, ketones flow to your brain in a smooth manner avoiding blood sugar swings in your body. This smooth flow ensures improvement in your mental concentration levels and focus apart from clearing away brain fog. This advantage is one of the main reasons why the keto diet is so popular across the globe. You can experience these boosted mental health advantages in the initial days when you start the keto diet. The sole cause is that your brain gets a steady, smooth, and regular supply of ketones instead of carbs, resulting in higher mental health.

Reversal of Type-2 Diabetes & Controlled Blood Sugar Levels:
It is an established scientific fact that the keto diet is effective in lowering the blood sugar content of the body and reduces the negative impact of having higher insulin levels. Logically, it can be concluded that the keto diet is more effective in letting you avoid type-2 diabetes in addition to reversal of pre-diabetic conditions. It is quite efficient in reversing type-2 diabetes, and you can find many studies to support this argument.

Improved Critical Health Markers:
As soon as your carb intake is lowered, health markers like cholesterol levels (both HDL and triglycerides), blood pressure levels, and blood sugar levels show a remarkable stability and improvement in them. These health markers are linked with improved weight, waist circumference, metabolic syndrome, and reversal of type-2 diabetes.

Improved Digestive System:

The keto diet is extremely useful in boosting your digestive performance. It lowers or removes any gas in your stomach apart from lowering down pain and cramps. The better state of your digestive system can be felt in the initial 2-3 days of the keto diet plan. Bloating and gas fare caused by FODMAP when the carbs inside it ferment in the lower intestine. This fluid isn't digested by the gut walls of the intestine and thus results in diarrhea. The ketogenic diet is devised as an anti-IBS approach and has a strictly low FODMAP. Your digestive system is vastly improved by the removal of carbs from your diet plan.

Improved Physical Endurance and Strength:
The regular, steady, and stimulated supply of energy via fats leads to a boosted physically strengthened body. The energy obtained from blood glucose (carbs) only lasts for a few hour of exercising. In comparison, energy obtained from fats is present in the body for weeks and months, thus making your body physically strong and enduring.

Treatment of Epilepsy:
Epilepsy has been treated very effectively by keto diet since the 1920s. Previously, the keto diet was only used on children having epilepsy, but now it has also been applied on adults due to its promising results. Epilepsy patients when starting the keto diet restrict their use of medication at all or a smaller amount of medication without having the dangers of having seizures. With the keto diet, patients of epilepsy also avoid the side effects of drugs by limiting drug intake and boosting their mental performance.

The most promising advantage of the keto diet for epilepsy patient is that they tend to limit or remove any medications at all and still control the disease without the dangers of having any seizures. The side effects of anti-epilepsy are very dangerous like drowsiness, loss of concentration. You can avoid them by simply taking the keto diet.

Additional Advantages

In addition to the above mentioned advantages, the keto diet offers special health benefits, which can be life- changing factors for certain individuals. As soon as you lower your carb intake, you can experience, controlled blood pressure, avoid acne related issues, control your migraine and even have assistance in various mental health issues. Some of the additional advantages of the keto diet are as follows:

1. Lower Acne issues
2. Reversal of PCOS (Polycystic Ovary Syndrome)
3. Fever issues of Heartburning
4. Lower Attacks of Migraine
5. Enhanced Treatment of Brain Cancer
6. Lower Sugar Cravings
7. Cure of Alzheimer
8. Controlled Blood Pressure Levels

Tips and Tricks for Making A Keto Lifestyle Easier

The keto diet isn't that complicated or hard to follow, but certain tips and tricks can enhance your diet plan. The keto diet is a lifestyle and the following tips and tricks make it healthier for you. They are as follows:

- **Tips for Breastfeeding Mothers:**

Never lower your carb intake from 50g carbs/day. Add 3-4 fruits to your keto plan and drink an ample amount of water for avoiding dehydration for better milk production. Consume fibers, veggies, and fats for and opt for a slightly moderate keto diet than a stricter one. Always visit a doctor in case of any complication.

- **Tips for Diabetics:**

It is not recommended for diabetics to follow the keto diet plan. In case you still want to adapt the plan, strictly check your blood sugar levels on a regular basis to keep them under the normal values. Also assess the ketone levels of your body to avoid Diabetic Ketoacidosis (DKA), which is a rare form of coma. Test your ketone levels when your blood sugar levels surpass the value of 240mg/dL as per the recommendations of American Diabetes Association (ADA).

- **Don't Obsess with the Weight Scale:**

The body's responses to the keto diet might vary from person to person and might not have a uniform effect on weight loss. Some people might take time in losing their fat, while others might lose weight instantly and drastically. One more thing to understand that the keto diet isn't solely about losing weight, so you shouldn't only focus your weight, but consider the other health benefits it offers, too.

- **Don't take Processed Fats:**

Vegetable oils and seeds are usually processed fats and a serious health danger for you. They are known to cause heart attacks, cancer, and increasing cholesterol levels, apart from various other health complications. You are recommended to avoid them at any cost.

- **Consume Enough Healthy Fats:**

Having a maintained and ample supply of fats is the integral part of the keto diet plan. It is usually very hard to sustain the supply of fats in the starting days of the kept diet plan. We recommend maintain this supply to get more from your diet plan.

- **Draft a Meal Plan:**

Having a properly and thoroughly drafted meal plan is the key to a successful keto diet. In case you don't plan your meals, you are not going to have the necessary amount of macros your body needs and will eventually end up consuming food, which is going to knock you out of your hard earned ketosis.

- **Don't take Excessive Proteins:**

The purpose of proteins in the keto diet is to maintain the mass, while fats are responsible for the energy supply of the body for its working. A higher intake of proteins is known to increase the blood sugar levels which are very harmful for your ketosis levels. Plan your diet properly to avoid ending up taking excessive proteins.

- **Keto is a Lifestyle:**

Don't just consider the keto diet as a diet only; rather, it's a complete lifestyle. If you stop following the diet as soon as you achieve your customized results, you are going to end up gradually from where you started. If you are following it just for the weight loss, simply reduce or restrict the sugar in your regular diet plan. The keto diet demands consistency, so adapt it properly.

- **Stop Comparisons:**

As mentioned earlier, the effects of keto diet may vary from person to person and is not necessarily uniform for everyone. Instead of focusing on how others have excelled with the keto diet isn't a suitable thing. Rather, target your diet properly and follow it perfectly to yield promising results.

- **Maintain your body's hydration levels:**

The keto diet might cause excessive sweating and various other effects, so it is recommended to drink an ample amount of water and other keto based drinks. This is going to keep your body hydrated and maintain your perfect, healthy shape.

- **Protein to Carb ratio:**

Keep your keto diet in proper proportions to have a perfect ketosis. The fat content of a keto diet is high, the protein intake is moderate and you are going to a lower carb intake while being on the keto diet plan. According to a rough sketch, your carb intake should be around 5% (the lower the better), the protein intake should comprise around 15-25% of proteins and the rest of the diet should comprise of 75% fats.

- **Tips for consuming more Fats:**

Usually, eggs and dairy is considered to be the main source of fats in the keto diet. Other fat sources on the keto diet include various plant-based oils which are usually used as an alternative for animal fats. These include:
1. Red Palm Oil
2. Olive Oil

3. Coconut Oil
4. MCT Oil
5. Avocado Oil

- **Tips for Drinking:**

Generally, we recommend drinking an ample supply of water as a key beverage for the keto diet. You can also drink coffee and tea on the keto diet by avoiding using any sweeteners, especially those with sugar in them. You can have a limited amount of cream or milk in your coffee but never go for a coffee latte. You can also drink a single glass of wine occasionally while on the keto diet plan.

Why 21 Days Meal Plan?

It is necessary to make a meal plan if you are beginning the keto diet. This meal plan will help you to lose weight if you follow it properly. Normally, the length of the week plans varies according to different diets. However, for the beginners of the keto diet, we recommend 21 days meal plan. This is a complete meal plan, along with the delicious and mouthwatering recipes, listed below. These recipes are tasty to eat and easy to cook for beginners of the keto diet. The 21 Days Meal Plan for Beginner's Keto Diet is as follows with the breakfast, lunch and dinner:

Day 1
Breakfast: Scrambled Eggs
Lunch: Mediterranean Spinach with Cheese
Dinner: Paprika Shrimp

Day 2
Breakfast: Pepperoni Omelet
Lunch: Parmesan Roasted Bamboo Sprouts
Dinner: Sweet and Sour Fish

Day 3
Breakfast: Eggs stuffed with Avocado and Watercress
Lunch: Green Beans with Mushrooms and Bacon
Dinner: Ketogenic Butter Fish

Day 4
Breakfast: Cheesy Mini Frittatas
Lunch: Bacon Wrapped Asparagus
Dinner: Omega-Rich Dinner

Day 5

Breakfast: Keto Coconut Pancakes
Lunch: Tomato Soup
Dinner: Buttered Scallops

Day 6
Breakfast: Nut Porridge
Lunch: Creamy Chicken Thighs
Dinner: BBQ Trout

Day 7
Breakfast: Lemon Mousse
Lunch: Cheesy Chicken Tenders
Dinner: Roasted Broccoli and Cauliflower

Day 8
Breakfast: Vanilla Yogurt
Lunch: Stuffed Whole Chicken
Dinner: Grilled Halloumi Salad

Day 9
Breakfast: Low Carb Blueberry Muffins
Lunch: Caprese Hasselback Chicken
Dinner: Mustard Pork Chops

Day 10
Breakfast: Keto Quiche
Lunch: Air Fried Chicken
Dinner: Bacon Swiss Pork Chops

Day 11
Breakfast: Tofu with Mushrooms
Lunch: Garlic Creamy Beef Steak
Dinner: Greek Pork Gyros

Day 12
Breakfast: Bacon Veggies Combo
Lunch: Beef Fajitas
Dinner: Roasted Pork

Day 13
Breakfast: Onion Tofu Scramble
Lunch: Beef Roast
Dinner: Dinner Pork Tenderloin

Day 14
Breakfast: Ham Spinach Ballet
Lunch: Beef Curry
Dinner: Broccoli Cheese Soup

Day 15
Breakfast: Bacon Bok Choy Samba
Lunch: 2-Meat Chili
Dinner: Cheesy Cauliflower

Day 16
Breakfast: Spinach Quiche
Lunch: Jamaican Jerk Pork Roast
Dinner: Mexican Cheesy Veggies

Day 17
Breakfast: Asparagus Bites
Lunch: Pork Carnitas
Dinner: Cheesy Brussels Sprout

Day 18
Breakfast: Scrambled Eggs

Lunch: Zesty Pork Chops
Dinner: Ketogenic Beef Sirloin Steak

Day 19
Breakfast: Cheesy Mini Frittatas
Lunch: Crispy Parmesan Crusted Pork Chops
Dinner: Mexican Taco Casserole

Day 20
Breakfast: Nut Porridge
Lunch: Fabulous Grilled Pork
Dinner: Keto Minced Meat

Day 21
Breakfast: Vanilla Yogurt
Lunch: Mahi Mahi Cakes
Dinner: Keto Low Carb Meatballs

My Experience with Diet

My experience with the keto diet has been transformative and drastically changed my lifestyle. I was recommended by a friend to switch to the keto diet for my excessive weight and belly fat. As soon as I transitioned to the keto diet, I experienced a few side effects for the starting days of the diet plan. These initial changes included keto breath, keto fever, keto flu, and dizziness. After a week, as my body adjusted to the process of ketosis, these side effects dissipated.

I understood that my body was in ketosis by having an increase in thirst, and a dry mouth. I also faced an increased need to urinate very often. I also experienced a steady boost in my energy levels and felt euphoric. My appetite was also stable, and I fewer food cravings. At the end of the 3rd week of my keto diet plan, I had lost around 25 lbs. of weight and was so proud and surprised!

Specifically, I lost this high amount of weight by following a perfect keto diet and a perfect ketosis. I restricted my carb intake to around 20 grams/day, took my protein intake according to a rough sketch of 1 gram of protein for every 1 kilogram of my body weight, in addition to consuming an ample amount of fats. In the meantime, I focused on avoiding snacking as much as I could when I wasn't hungry. This trick enabled me to keep my ketosis at a strong pace and avert any slowdowns. I also engaged in intermittent fasting during this time period, by eating for 8 hours during the day and fasting for the next 16 hours. I also maintained a strong routine of working out and regular exercising and attained regular sleep of around 7-8 hours. These results may vary from person to person, as the bodies react differently to the keto diet. But, one thing is for sure: the keto diet is the best diet plan to achieve a healthy weight loss approach and obtain a healthy and nutritious lifestyle!

Vegetables and Side Dishes Recipes

Broccoli Cheese Soup

Serves: 6
Prep Time: 5 hours 10 mins
This great and flavorful soup is a flavor bomb!

Ingredients
- 1 cup heavy whipping cream
- 2 cups chicken broth
- 2 cups broccoli
- Salt, to taste
- 2 cups cheddar cheese

Directions
1) Place the cheddar cheese, broccoli, chicken broth, heavy whipping cream and salt in a crock pot.
2) Set the crock pot on LOW and cook for about 5 hours.
3) Ladle out in a bowl and serve hot.

Nutrition
Calories: 244 Carbs: 3.4g Fats: 20.4g Proteins: 12.3g Sodium: 506mg Sugar: 1g

Mediterranean Spinach with Cheese

Serves: 6
Prep Time: 25 mins

This Mediterranean dish is perfect for serving at luncheons or special gatherings with your favorite drink.

Ingredients

- 2 pounds spinach, chopped
- ½ cup black olives, halved and pitted
- Salt and black pepper, to taste
- 4 tablespoons butter
- 1½ cups feta cheese, grated
- 4 teaspoons fresh lemon zest, grated

Directions

1) Preheat the Air fryer to 400 degrees F and grease an Air fryer basket.
2) Cook spinach for about 4 minutes in a pan of boiling water. Drain well.
3) Mix together butter, spinach, salt, and black pepper in a bowl.
4) Transfer the spinach mixture into an air fryer basket.
5) Cook for about 15 minutes, tossing once in the middle way.
6) Dish into a bowl and stir in the olives, cheese, and lemon zest to serve.

Nutrition

Calories: 215 Carbs: 8g Fats: 17.5g Proteins: 9.9g Sodium: 690mg Sugar: 2.3g

Cheesy Cauliflower

Serves: 6
Prep Time: 30 mins

Cheese adds to the richness of the dish. Use any type of cheese you like. I prefer Parmesan!

Ingredients
- 2 tablespoons mustard
- ½ cup butter, cut into small pieces
- 2 cauliflower heads, chopped
- 1 cup Parmesan cheese, grated
- 2 teaspoons avocado mayonnaise

Directions
1) Preheat the oven to 400 degrees F and grease a baking dish.
2) Mix together mustard and avocado mayonnaise in a bowl.
3) Coat the cauliflower with the mustard mixture and transfer into a baking dish.
4) Top with Parmesan cheese and butter and bake for about 25 minutes.
5) Pull from the oven and serve hot.

Nutrition
Calories: 201 Carbs: 6.2g Fats: 18.9g Proteins: 4.3g Sodium: 192mg Sugar: 2.4g

Parmesan Roasted Bamboo Sprouts

Serves: 6
Prep Time: 25 mins

These delicious and ketogenic Parmesan Roasted Bamboo Sprouts will leave you begging for more.

Ingredients
- 2 cups Parmesan cheese, grated
- 2 pounds bamboo sprouts
- 4 tablespoons butter
- ½ teaspoon paprika
- Salt and black pepper, to taste

Directions
1) Preheat the oven to 365 degrees F and grease a baking dish.
2) Marinate the bamboo sprouts with paprika, butter, salt, and black pepper, and keep aside.
3) Transfer the seasoned bamboo sprouts in the baking dish and place in the oven.
4) Bake for about 15 minutes and dish to serve.

Nutrition
Calories: 162 Carbs: 4.7g Fats: 11.7g Proteins: 7.5g Sodium: 248mg Sugar: 1.4g

Mexican Cheesy Veggies

Serves: 4
Prep Time: 40 mins

This recipe comprises a delicious combo of fresh veggies, with herbs and Mexican cheese.

Ingredients
- 1 onion, thinly sliced
- 1 tomato, thinly sliced
- 1 zucchini, sliced
- 1 teaspoon mixed dried herbs
- Salt and black pepper, to taste
- 1 teaspoon olive oil
- 1 cup Mexican cheese, grated

Directions
1) Preheat the oven to 370 degrees F and grease a baking dish.
2) Layer the vegetables in the baking dish and drizzle with olive oil.
3) Top evenly with cheese and sprinkle with herbs, salt, and black pepper.
4) Bake for about 30 minutes and dish to serve hot.

Nutrition
Calories: 305 Carbs: 8.3g Fats: 22.3g Proteins: 15.2g Sodium: 370mg Sugar: 4.2g

Green Beans with Mushrooms and Bacons

Serves: 4
Prep Time: 25 mins

Green beans, along with juicy mushrooms, provide a great source of nutrients and satisfy your appetite fully.

Ingredients
- 4 tablespoons onion, minced
- 4 tablespoons butter
- 1 teaspoon garlic, minced
- 4 cooked bacon slices, crumbled
- 2 cups frozen green beans
- 2 (8-ounce) package white mushrooms, sliced
- ¼ teaspoon salt

Directions
1) Put the butter, onions and garlic in the Instant Pot and select "Sauté."
2) Sauté for about 2 minutes and add in bacon and salt.
3) Close the lid and cook at "High" and "Manual" pressure for about 10 minutes.
4) Select "Cancel" and carefully do a natural release.
5) Remove the lid and stir in beans and mushrooms.
6) Lock the lid again and cook at "High" and "Manual" pressure for about 7 minutes.
7) Transfer to a bowl and serve hot.

Nutrition
Calories: 220 Carbs: 11.6g Fats: 17g Proteins: 10g Sodium: 488mg Sugar: 3.2g

Cauliflower Mash

Serves: 4
Prep Time: 20 mins

It is a great change from mashed potatoes and just as versatile.

Ingredients

- 1 tablespoon full-fat coconut milk
- 3 garlic cloves, minced
- 1 teaspoon green chilies, chopped
- 3 tablespoons butter
- ½ cup feta cheese
- 1 head cauliflower stems, completely removed
- Salt and black pepper, to taste

Directions

1) Preheat the oven to 360 degrees F and grease a baking dish.
2) Place cauliflower pieces in the baking dish and transfer into the oven.
3) Bake for about 10 minutes and dish out the cauliflower pieces.
4) Mix with the remaining ingredients and blend with an immersion hand blender to achieve the desired texture.

Nutrition

Calories: 154 Carbs: 5.3g Fats: 13.5g Proteins: 4.3g Sodium: 292mg Sugar: 2.5g

Bacon Wrapped Asparagus

Serves: 3
Prep Time: 30 mins

This simple recipe is delicious, easy, and satisfying, especially for those on a ketogenic or low-carb diet.

Ingredients
- 6 small asparagus spears
- 3 bacon slices
- 2 tablespoons butter
- ¼ cup heavy whipping cream
- Salt and black pepper, to taste

Directions
1) Preheat the oven to 370 degrees F and grease the baking dish with butter.
2) Sprinkle the asparagus spears with salt and black pepper.
3) Add heavy whipping cream to the asparagus and wrap with bacon slices.
4) Place the wrapped asparagus in the baking dish and transfer into the oven.
5) Bake for about 20 minutes and dish out to serve hot.

Nutrition
Calories: 176 Carbs: 1.2g Fats: 13.4g Proteins: 0.8g Sodium: 321mg Sugar: 0.5g

Cheesy Brussels Sprout

Serves: 5
Prep Time: 35 mins

Mouth-watering creamy cheesy sauce slathered over Brussels sprouts are so soft, your teeth will slide through them.

Ingredients
- 1 pound Brussels sprouts
- 3 tablespoons olive oil
- ½ cup cream
- Salt and black pepper, to taste
- 2 tablespoons butter
- ½ cup parmesan cheese, grated

Directions
1) Preheat the oven to 360 degrees F and grease a baking dish.
2) Mix together Brussels sprouts, olive oil, parmesan cheese, salt, and black pepper in a bowl.
3) Transfer the Brussels sprouts in the baking dish and drizzle with butter.
4) Transfer it into the oven and bake for about 25 minutes.
5) Dish to serve hot.

Nutrition
Calories: 190 Carbs: 8.5g Fats: 16.8g Proteins: 5g Sodium: 124mg Sugar: 2g

Tomato Soup

Serves: 4
Prep Time: 30 mins

Everybody that tries this dish loves it. You may need to double this recipe to have enough!

Ingredients
- 2 cups low-sodium vegetable broth
- ¼ cup fresh basil, chopped
- 1 garlic clove, minced
- 1 teaspoon dried parsley, crushed
- Freshly ground black pepper, to taste
- 1 teaspoon dried basil, crushed
- 2 tablespoons Erthyritol
- ½ tablespoon balsamic vinegar
- ½ tablespoon olive oil
- 1 pound fresh tomatoes, chopped
- 1 cup cheddar cheese

Directions
1) Put the oil in a pot and add tomatoes, garlic, herbs, black pepper, and broth.
2) Cover the lid and cook for about 18-20 minutes on medium-low heat.
3) Stir in sugar and vinegar and place the mixture in an immersion blender.
4) Blend until smooth and ladle into a bowl.
5) Garnish with basil and serve immediately.

Nutrition
Calories: 194 Carbs: 5.6g Fats: 15.4g Proteins: 9.2g Sodium: 257mg Sugar: 3.2g

Poultry Recipes

Creamy Chicken Thighs

Serves: 4
Prep Time: 30 mins

It is slightly time consuming, but it is worth the wait. Select a chicken sized according to the amount of people you will be serving.

Ingredients
- 1 small onion
- 2 tablespoons butter
- 1 pound chicken thighs
- ½ cup sour cream
- Salt, to taste

Directions
1) Season the chicken thighs generously with salt and keep aside.
2) Put butter and onions in a skillet on medium-low heat and sauté for about 3 minutes.
3) Add chicken thighs and cover the lid.
4) Cook for about 10 minutes and stir in the sour cream.
5) Cook for about 5 minutes and dish out to serve hot.

Nutrition
Calories: 447 Carbs: 3.8g Fats: 26.9g Proteins: 45.3g Sodium: 206mg Sugar: 1.1g

Ham Stuffed Turkey Rolls

Serves: 4
Prep Time: 30 mins

This is an easy recipe. Customize until your heart's content. Great for snacks!

Ingredients
- 2 tablespoons fresh sage leaves
- Salt and black pepper, to taste
- 4 ham slices
- 4 (6-ounce) turkey cutlets
- 1 tablespoon butter, melted

Directions
1) Season the turkey cutlets with salt and black pepper.
2) Roll the turkey cutlets and wrap ham slices tightly around each cutlet.
3) Coat each roll with butter and place the sage leaves evenly.
4) Heat a non-stick pan and cook ham stuffed turkey rolls for about 10 minutes on each side.
5) Dish out and serve immediately.

Nutrition
Calories: 467 Carbs: 1.7g Fats: 24.8g Proteins: 56g Sodium: 534mg Sugar: 0g

Cheesy Chicken Tenders

Serves: 6
Prep Time: 25 mins

This recipe is forgiving. I eyeballed everything until it was how I wanted it, so these measurements aren't exact.

Ingredients
- 1 cup cream
- 1 cup feta cheese
- 4 tablespoons butter
- 2 pounds chicken tenders
- Salt and black pepper, to taste

Directions
1) Preheat the oven to 360 degrees F and grease a baking dish.
2) Season chicken tenders with salt and black pepper and keep aside.
3) Heat butter in a non-stick pan and add chicken tenders.
4) Cook for about 5 minutes on each side and transfer to the baking dish.
5) Top with cream and feta cheese and bake for about 15 minutes.
6) Place onto a platter and serve hot.

Nutrition
Calories: 447 Carbs: 2.3g Fats: 26.4g Proteins: 47.7g Sodium: 477mg Sugar: 1.8g

Chili Lime Turkey

Serves: 6
Prep Time: 20 mins

This is a quick and easy turkey dinner with the perfect combination of chili and lime.

Ingredients
- ¼ cup cooking wine
- ½ teaspoon paprika
- 5 garlic cloves, minced
- 1 tablespoon lime juice
- ¼ cup butter
- 1 onion, diced
- 1 teaspoon sea salt
- ½ cup organic chicken broth
- 2 pounds turkey thighs
- 1 teaspoon dried parsley
- 3 green chilies, chopped

Directions
1) Put butter, onions, and garlic in a large skillet and sauté for about 3 minutes.
2) Add rest of the ingredients and cook for about 20 minutes.
3) Dish out in a platter and serve hot.

Nutrition
Calories: 282 Carbs: 6.3g Fats: 15.2g Proteins: 27.4g Sodium: 2117mg Sugar: 3.3g

Stuffed Whole Chicken

Serves: 6
Prep Time: 8 hours 10 mins

It is easy to prepare ahead of time for a very quick meal in a pinch.

Ingredients

- 1 cup Monterey Jack cheese
- 4 whole garlic cloves, peeled
- 1 (2-pound) whole chicken, cleaned, pat dried
- Salt and black pepper, to taste
- 2 tablespoons fresh lemon juice

Directions

1) Stuff the chicken cavity with Monterey Jack cheese and garlic cloves.
2) Season the chicken with salt and black pepper.
3) Transfer the chicken into the slow cooker and drizzle with lemon juice.
4) Set the slow cooker on LOW and cook for about 8 hours.
5) Dish out and serve hot.

Nutrition

Calories: 309 Carbs: 1.6g Fats: 12.1g Proteins: 45.8g Sodium: 201mg Sugar: 0.7g

Mediterranean Turkey Cutlets

Serves: 4
Prep Time: 25 mins

I came up with this one to place a new twist on the classic, beloved turkey.

Ingredients
- 2 tablespoons olive oil
- 1 pound turkey cutlets
- ½ cup almond flour
- 1 teaspoon turmeric powder
- 1 teaspoon Greek seasoning

Directions
1) Mix together Greek seasoning, almond flour, and turmeric powder in a bowl and coat turkey cutlets with this mixture.
2) Heat oil in a skillet and add the turkey cutlets.
3) Cover the lid and cook for about 20 minutes on medium-low heat.
4) Dish out in a serving platter and serve.

Nutrition
Calories: 340 Carbs: 3.7g Fats: 19.4g Proteins: 36.3g Sodium: 124mg Sugar: 0g

Caprese Hasselback Chicken

Serves: 4
Prep Time: 25 mins

Caprese Hasselback Chicken is yet another mouth-watering and delicious recipe, providing your body all the energy you need.

Ingredients
- 4 large chicken breasts
- 2 tablespoons butter
- 1 cup fresh mozzarella cheese, thinly sliced
- 2 large roma tomatoes, thinly sliced
- Salt and freshly ground black pepper, to taste

Directions
1) Make slits in the chicken breasts and season with salt and black pepper.
2) Stuff the mozzarella cheese slices and tomatoes in the chicken slits.
3) Preheat the oven to 365 degrees F and grease the baking dish with butter.
4) Arrange the stuffed chicken breasts in the baking dish and transfer into the oven.
5) Bake for about 1 hour and dish to serve.

Nutrition
Calories: 287 Carbs: 3.8g Fats: 15g Proteins: 33.2g Sodium: 178mg Sugar: 2.4g

Keto Garlic Turkey Breasts

Serves: 4
Prep Time: 25 mins

This recipe makes your turkey moist and full of flavor. You can also use this recipe for chicken breasts, Cornish game hens, or roasting chicken.

Ingredients
- 4 tablespoons butter
- ½ teaspoon garlic powder
- ¼ teaspoon dried oregano
- ½ teaspoon salt
- 1 pound turkey breasts, boneless
- ¼ teaspoon dried basil
- 1 teaspoon black pepper

Directions
1) Preheat the oven to 420 degrees F and grease a baking tray.
2) Season the turkey with garlic powder, dried oregano, salt, dried basil, and black pepper.
3) Put butter and seasoned turkey in a skillet and cook for about 4 minutes on each side.
4) Transfer the turkey in the oven and bake for about 15 minutes.
5) Dish out in a platter and serve hot.

Nutrition
Calories: 223 Carbs: 5.4g Fats: 13.4g Proteins: 19.6g Sodium: 1524mg Sugar: 4.1g

Air Fried Chicken

Serves: 4
Prep Time: 20 mins

By using Air fryer, we get a recipe the family loves and is practically ketogenic! Serve with blue cheese or ranch dressing.

Ingredients
- 2 tablespoons olive oil
- 8 skinless, boneless chicken tenderloins
- 2 eggs
- Salt and black pepper, to taste
- 1 teaspoon turmeric powder

Directions
1) Preheat the air fryer to 360 degrees F and coat the basket with olive oil.
2) Whisk together eggs in a bowl and dip the tenderloins in it.
3) Mix together turmeric powder, salt, and black pepper in a bowl and dredge the chicken tenderloins in it.
4) Transfer the tenderloins in the fryer basket and cook for about 10 minutes.
5) Dish out and serve with tomato ketchup or any dip of your choice.

Nutrition
Calories: 342 Carbs: 0.4g Fats: 14.9g Proteins: 50g Sodium: 80mg Sugar: 0g

Creamy Turkey Breast

Serves: 6
Prep Time: 2 hours 10 mins

A great new way to try turkey! The sour cream seals in the moisture, and no one would ever guess that it is in there.

Ingredients
- 2 tablespoons butter
- ½ cup sour cream
- 1½ cups Italian dressing
- 1 (2-pound) bone-in turkey breast
- 2 garlic cloves, minced
- Salt and black pepper, to taste

Directions
1) Preheat the oven to 360 degrees F and grease a baking dish with butter.
2) Mix together garlic cloves, salt, and black pepper. Then rub the turkey breast with this mixture.
3) Transfer the turkey breast in the baking dish and top with sour cream and Italian dressing.
4) Bake for about 2 hours, coating with pan juices intermittently.
5) Dish out and serve immediately.

Nutrition
Calories: 369 Carbs: 6.5g Fats: 23.2g Proteins: 35.4g Sodium: 990mg Sugar: 4.9g

Beef Recipes

Garlic Creamy Beef Steak

Serves: 6
Prep Time: 45 mins
This is a simple and easy dish, with healthy ingredients.

Ingredients
- 4 garlic cloves, minced
- ½ cup butter
- 2 pounds beef top sirloin steaks
- 1½ cup cream
- Salt and freshly ground black pepper, to taste

Directions
1) Rub the beef top sirloin steaks with garlic, salt and black pepper.
2) Marinate the beef with cream and butter and keep aside.
3) Preheat the grill and transfer the steaks on it.
4) Grill for about 15 minutes on each side and serve hot.

Nutrition
Calories: 353 Carbs: 3.9g Fats: 24.1g Proteins: 31.8g Sodium: 298mg Sugar: 1.2g

Ketogenic Beef Sirloin Steak

Serves: 3
Prep Time: 35 mins

All ingredients included in this dish assists with weight loss. It includes beef, which gives high nutrition to the body.

Ingredients
- ½ teaspoon garlic powder
- 3 tablespoons butter
- 1 pound beef top sirloin steaks
- 1 garlic clove, minced
- Salt and freshly ground black pepper, to taste

Directions
1) Put butter and beef sirloin steaks in a large grill pan.
2) Cook for about 2 minutes on each side to brown the steaks.
3) Add garlic clove, garlic powder, salt, and black pepper and cook for about 15 minutes on each side on medium-high heat.
4) Transfer the steaks in a serving platter and serve hot.

Nutrition
Calories: 246 Carbs: 2g Fats: 13.1g Proteins: 31.3g Sodium: 224mg Sugar: 0.1g

Beef Fajitas

Serves: 3
Prep Time: 8 hours 20 mins

Traditional fajitas with a colorful twist of flavor! These yummy, steak filled, beef fajitas are sure to tingle your taste buds.

Ingredients
- 1 bell pepper, sliced
- 1 tablespoon butter
- 1 pound beef, sliced
- 1 onion, sliced
- 1 tablespoon fajita seasoning

Directions
1) Place the butter in the bottom of the slow cooker and add onions, fajita seasoning, bell pepper, and beef.
2) Set the slow cooker on LOW and cook for about 8 hours.
3) Dish out the delicious beef fajitas and serve hot.

Nutrition
Calories: 353 Carbs: 8.5g Fats: 13.4g Proteins: 46.7g Sodium: 304mg Sugar: 3.6g

Mexican Taco Casserole

Serves: 3
Prep Time: 40 mins
It is easy to make ahead and serve quickly for a filling meal.

Ingredients
- ½ cup cottage cheese
- ½ cup cheddar cheese, shredded
- 1 pound ground beef
- 1 tablespoon taco seasoning
- ½ cup salsa

Directions
1) Mix together the ground beef and taco seasoning in a bowl.
2) Stir in the cottage cheese, cheddar cheese and salsa.
3) Preheat the oven to 400 degrees F and grease a baking dish.
4) Transfer the ground beef mixture in the baking dish and top with cheese mixture.
5) Bake for about 30 minutes and serve warm.

Nutrition
Calories: 409 Carbs: 5.7g Fats: 16.5g Proteins: 56.4g Sodium: 769mg Sugar: 1.9g

Beef Roast

Serves: 6
Prep Time: 1 hour

Flavorful beef broth and onion soup serve double-duty in this tasty recipe, as they are used as a basting sauce for the roast.

Ingredients
- 1 cup onion soup
- 2 pounds beef roast
- 1 cups beef broth
- Salt and freshly ground black pepper, to taste

Directions
1) Put the beef roast in the pressure cooker and then add beef broth, onion soup, salt, and black pepper.
2) Secure the lid and cook at high pressure for about 50 minutes.
3) Release the pressure naturally and dish onto a serving platter.

Nutrition
Calories: 349 Carbs: 2.9g Fats: 18.8g Proteins: 39.9g Sodium: 480mg Sugar: 1.2g

Keto Minced Meat

Serves: 4
Prep Time: 30 mins

This is a minced meat recipe, which is easy to prepare and wonderful to eat.

Ingredients
- 1 pound ground lamb meat
- 2 tablespoons butter
- 1 cup onions, chopped
- ½ teaspoon turmeric powder
- 1 teaspoon salt
- ½ teaspoon cayenne pepper
- 1 tablespoon garlic, minced
- 1 tablespoon ginger, minced
- ½ teaspoon ground coriander
- ½ teaspoon cumin powder

Directions
1) Put the butter, garlic, ginger, and onions in a pot and sauté for about 3 minutes.
2) Add ground meat and all the spices. Next, lock the lid.
3) Cook for about 20 minutes on medium-high heat and present in a large serving bowl.

Nutrition
Calories: 304 Carbs: 4.8g Fats: 21.1g Proteins: 21.8g Sodium: 705mg Sugar: 1.3g

Beef Curry

Serves: 9
Prep Time: 2 hours

This beef curry has been a family favorite for years. Serve over steamed white rice.

Ingredients
- 2½ pounds chuck roast, cubed into 1-inch size
- ½ cup beef broth
- Salt and black pepper, to taste
- 3 tablespoons Thai red curry paste
- 2 tablespoons butter
- 2½ cups coconut milk
- ¼ cup fresh cilantro, chopped

Directions
1) Put butter and curry paste in a large pan on low heat.
2) Sauté for about 3 minutes and stir in coconut milk and beef broth.
3) Simmer for about 5 minutes and add beef.
4) Cook for about 5 minutes on high heat until boiled.
5) Lower the heat and simmer, covered for about 1 hour while occasionally stirring.
6) Transfer the beef into a bowl with a slotted spoon and keep the pan aside.
7) Remove the fats from top of the curry and return the pan to medium heat.
8) Stir in the beef and simmer for about 30 minutes on low heat.
9) Garnish with cilantro and season with salt to serve.

Nutrition
Calories: 470 Carbs: 4.8g Fats: 30.5g Proteins: 43.5g Sodium: 414mg Sugar: 2.3g

Grilled Beef Steak

Serves: 6
Prep Time: 25 mins

Feel free to garnish this beef steak with cheese, sour cream, salsa, Mexican queso, and crema fresca when serving.

Ingredients
- 2 teaspoons dried rosemary, crushed
- 2 pounds beef top sirloin steaks
- ¼ cup unsalted butter
- 3 garlic cloves, minced
- Salt and black pepper, to taste

Directions
1) Preheat the grill and grease the grill grate.
2) Rub the steaks generously with rosemary, salt, and black pepper.
3) Grill the steaks for about 5 minutes on each side.
4) Melt butter in a pan on medium-low heat and add garlic.
5) Transfer the steaks in serving plates and coat the steaks evenly with melted butter.
6) Keep aside for about 5 minutes and serve hot.

Nutrition
Calories: 352 Carbs: 0.8g Fats: 17.2g Proteins: 46.1g Sodium: 155mg Sugar: 0g

2-Meat Chili

Serves: 8
Prep Time: 45 mins

This is a really scrumptious recipe. It is super easy and everyone loves it.

Ingredients
- 1 pound grass-fed ground beef
- ½ of small yellow onion, chopped
- 2 garlic cloves, minced
- 1 tablespoon ground cumin
- Salt and freshly ground black pepper, to taste
- ½ cup cheddar cheese, shredded
- 1 tablespoon olive oil
- 1 pound ground pork
- 3 medium tomatillos, chopped
- 2 jalapeño peppers, chopped
- 1 (6-ounce) can sugar-free tomato sauce
- 1 tablespoon chili powder
- ¼ cup water

Directions
1) Heat the oil in a pressure cooker and add beef and pork.
2) Cook for about 5 minutes on medium heat and add the remaining ingredients, except cheese.
3) Lock the lid and cook for about 30 minutes at high pressure.
4) Release the pressure naturally and top with cheddar cheese.

Nutrition
Calories: 259 Carbs: 5.4g Fats: 12.5g Proteins: 29.9g Sodium: 253mg Sugar: 1.2g

Keto Low Carb Meat Balls

Serves: 6
Prep Time: 35 mins

These homemade low carb meatballs are very easy to make and are downright simple.

Ingredients
- 2 tablespoons Parmesan cheese, grated
- 1 egg
- Salt and ground black pepper to taste
- 1 (14 ounce) can tomato sauce
- 2 pounds ground beef
- 1 teaspoon dried oregano
- 2 tablespoons olive oil
- 1 tablespoon flaxseed meal
- ½ cup water

Directions
1) Mix ground beef, flaxseed, oregano, Parmesan cheese, egg, salt, and black pepper in a bowl until well mixed.
2) Roll the mixture into small balls and keep aside.
3) Heat oil in a non-stick skillet and add meatballs in batches until brown in color.
4) Add water and cook for about 8 minutes on medium-low heat.
5) Dish in a bowl and serve hot.

Nutrition
Calories: 384 Carbs: 4.4g Fats: 17.3g Proteins: 50.9g Sodium: 543mg Sugar: 2.9g

Pork Recipes

Jamaican Jerk Pork Roast

Serves: 3
Prep Time: 35 mins

Fragrant, succulent, and savory pork shoulder roast that the whole family will love!

Ingredients
- 1 pound pork shoulder
- 1 tablespoon butter
- 1/8 cup Jamaican jerk spice blend
- 1/8 cup beef broth

Directions
1) Season the pork with Jamaican jerk spice blend.
2) Put the butter and seasoned pork in the pot and cook for about 5 minutes.
3) Add beef broth and lock the lid.
4) Cook for about 20 minutes on low heat and dish out in a serving platter.

Nutrition
Calories: 477 Carbs: 0g Fats: 36.2g Proteins: 35.4g Sodium: 162mg Sugar: 0g

Bacon Swiss Pork Chops

Serves: 4
Prep Time: 25 mins

This is a very delicious recipe. The main ingredient is beef. Beef gives energy to the body, and all the nutrition it needs.

Ingredients
- 4 pork chops, bone-in
- ½ cup Swiss cheese, shredded
- 6 bacon strips, cut in half
- 1 tablespoon butter
- Salt and freshly ground black pepper, to taste

Directions
1) Season the pork chops with salt and black pepper.
2) Put butter and seasoned pork chops in the skillet and cook for about 6 minutes.
3) Stir in bacon strips and cook for about 8 minutes.
4) Top with Swiss cheese and cook on low heat for about 5 minutes.
5) Remove from heat and dish on a platter.

Nutrition
Calories: 483 Carbs: 0.7g Fats: 40g Proteins: 27.7g Sodium: 552mg Sugar: 0.2g

Pork Carnitas

Serves: 3
Prep Time: 25 mins

Serve these pork carnitas with mashed sweet potatoes and cumin scented black beans to enhance the taste.

Ingredients
- 1 orange, juiced
- 1 tablespoon butter
- 1 pound pork shoulder, bone-in
- ½ teaspoon garlic powder
- Salt and freshly ground black pepper, to taste

Directions
1) Season the pork with salt and black pepper.
2) Put butter and garlic powder in the pot and sauté for about 1 minute.
3) Add seasoned pork and sauté for about 3 minutes.
4) Pour orange juice and secure the lid.
5) Cook for about 15 minutes on medium-high heat and dish out.
6) Shred with the help of a fork and immediately serve.

Nutrition
Calories: 506 Carbs: 7.6g Fats: 36.3g Proteins: 35.9g Sodium: 130mg Sugar: 5.8g

Mustard Pork Chops

Serves: 4
Prep Time: 40 mins

This is a simple and flavorful recipe. For best results, marinate the pork at least 8 hours and flip it after 4 hours.

Ingredients
- 2 tablespoons Dijon mustard
- 2 tablespoons butter
- 4 pork chops
- 1 tablespoon fresh rosemary, coarsely chopped
- Salt and freshly ground black pepper, to taste

Directions
1) Marinate the pork chops with fresh rosemary, Dijon mustard, salt, and black pepper for about 3 hours.
2) Put the butter and marinated pork chops in a non-stick skillet and cover the lid.
3) Cook for about 30 minutes on medium-low heat and dish to serve hot.

Nutrition
Calories: 315 Carbs: 1g Fats: 26.1g Proteins: 18.4g Sodium: 186mg Sugar: 0.1g

Zesty Pork Chops

Serves: 4
Prep Time: 35 mins

These pork chops with a sweet, tangy, and zesty glaze make it highly palatable and mouthwatering.

Ingredients
- 3 tablespoons lemon juice
- 4 tablespoons butter
- 4 pork chops, bone-in
- 1 cup picante sauce
- 2 tablespoons low-carb flour mix

Directions
1) Mix picante sauce and orange in a bowl and keep aside.
2) Coat the chops with flour and keep aside.
3) Put the oil and pork chops in the pressure cooker.
4) Close the lid and cook for about 15 minutes at high pressure.
5) Naturally release the pressure for 10 minutes and dish to serve hot.

Nutrition
Calories: 284 Carbs: 1g Fats: 19.5g Proteins: 24.8g Sodium: 150mg Sugar: 0.3g

Greek Pork Gyros

Serves: 4
Prep Time: 40 mins

This recipe is a delicious way for you to experience with the infusion of different herbs.

Ingredients
- 1 pound pork meat, ground
- 4 garlic cloves
- 1 teaspoon rosemary
- ¾ teaspoons salt
- ¼ teaspoon black pepper
- ½ small onion, chopped
- 1 teaspoon dried oregano
- 1 teaspoon ground marjoram
- ¾ cup water

Directions
1) Put onions, ground lamb meat, garlic, marjoram, rosemary, salt, and black pepper in a food processor and process until well combined.
2) Press Meat mixture into the Loaf Pan until very tight and compact.
3) Cover tightly with tin foil and poke some holes in the foil.
4) Preheat the oven to 390 degrees F and transfer the loaf pan in the oven.
5) Bake for about 25 minutes and dish to serve hot.

Nutrition
Calories: 242 Carbs: 2.4g Fats: 15.2g Proteins: 21.4g Sodium: 521mg Sugar: 0.4g

Crispy Parmesan Crusted Pork Chops

Serves: 4
Prep Time: 30 mins

These pork chops' delicious, Parmesan cheese crust are highly delicious and addictive.

Ingredients

- ½ teaspoon salt
- ½ teaspoon onion powder
- 4 thick pork chops, center cut boneless
- ¼ teaspoon pepper
- 1 teaspoon smoked paprika
- ¼ teaspoon chili powder
- 1 cup pork rind crumbs
- 2 large eggs
- 3 tablespoons parmesan cheese, grated

Directions

1) Preheat the Air fryer to 400 degrees F.
2) Season pork chops with salt and black pepper.
3) Mix together parmesan cheese, pork rind crumbs, and seasonings in a bowl.
4) Whisk the eggs in another bowl and dip each pork chop into the egg mixture first, and then in the crumb mixture.
5) Place pork chops in the air fryer basket and cook for about 20 minutes.
6) Dish out and serve with your favorite dip.

Nutrition

Calories: 271 Carbs: 1.2g Fats: 12.3g Proteins: 38.5g Sodium: 605mg Sugar: 0.4g

Roasted Pork

Serves: 12
Prep Time: 2 hours 25 mins

This is savory and tender roasted pork is great with rice and Asian veggies like bok choy!

Ingredients
- 2 teaspoons garlic powder
- ½ teaspoon sea salt
- 4 pounds pork
- 3 teaspoons thyme, dried
- 1 tablespoon Chimichurri sauce, for serving

Directions
1) Preheat the oven at 360 degrees F and wrap a baking sheet with foil.
2) Season the lamb breast with garlic powder, dried thyme, and salt.
3) Arrange the lamb onto the baking sheet and bake for about 1 hour.
4) Increase the temperature of the oven to 440 degrees F and transfer the baking sheet inside the oven.
5) Cook for about 1 hour and dish out the lamb breast onto a serving plate.
6) Top with lemon wedges and chimichurri sauce before serving hot.

Nutrition
Calories: 286 Carbs: 0.6g Fats: 11.3g Proteins: 42.6g Sodium: 200mg Sugar: 0.1g

Fabulous Grilled Pork

Serves: 12
Prep Time: 27 mins

This is always a winner! There are never any leftovers the next day!

Ingredients
- 2 garlic cloves, minced
- 2 tablespoons paprika
- 2 teaspoons fresh lemon zest, grated finely
- 2 tablespoons red chili powder
- 2 tablespoons ground coffee
- 4 (1½-pound) grass-fed pork
- Salt and freshly ground black pepper, to taste

Directions
1) Preheat the grill and grease the grill grate.
2) Mix together all the ingredients, except steaks, in a bowl and marinate the steaks in this mixture for about 1 hour.
3) Grill the steaks for about 7 minutes on each side.
4) Remove from grill onto a cutting board and cut the steaks in desired slices.
5) Serve hot.

Nutrition
Calories: 457 Carbs: 1.6g Fats: 20.7g Proteins: 62.4g Sodium: 174mg Sugar: 0.2g

Dinner Pork Tenderloin

Serves: 6
Prep Time: 1 hour 10 mins

This dish can be made at special occasions and provides all nutrition a body needs.

Ingredients
- 3 garlic cloves, minced
- Salt and freshly ground black pepper, to taste
- 1 (2-pound) grass-fed center-cut pork tenderloin roast
- 1 tablespoon fresh rosemary, minced and divided
- 1 tablespoon olive oil

Directions
1) Preheat the oven to 400 degrees F and grease a large shallow roasting pan.
2) Place beef into the roasting pan and mix with the garlic, rosemary, salt, and black pepper.
3) Drizzle with oil and roast for about 1 hour.
4) Remove from the oven and cut the tenderloin in desired slices to serve hot.

Nutrition
Calories: 343 Carbs: 0.9g Fats: 18g Proteins: 42g Sodium: 93mg Sugar: 0g

Fish and Seafood Recipes

Mahi Mahi Cakes

Serves: 4
Prep Time: 30 mins

Mahi Mahi cake is a highly scrumptious recipe. Mahi Mahi is the main ingredient of this recipe and filled with numerous benefits.

Ingredients
- 2 teaspoons primal palate seafood seasoning
- 12 oz. mahi mahi, canned
- ¼ cup onions, minced
- 3 tablespoons organic palm oil
- 2 teaspoons parsley, garnish
- 3 pasture egg yolks
- 1 teaspoon chives, garnish
- 4 lemon wedges, for garnish

Directions
1) Preheat the oven at 360 degrees F and grease a baking tray.
2) Mix together seafood seasoning, salmon, onions, and egg yolks in a bowl.
3) Make small patties out of this mixture and arrange them on the baking tray.
4) Transfer it in the oven and bake for about 15 minutes.
5) Dish out the patties and keep aside.
6) Put palm oil in a skillet on a medium-high heat and add patties.
7) Flip the sides of the patties and dish onto a plate.
8) Garnish with parsley, lemon wedges, and chives to serve.

Nutrition
Calories: 248 Carbs: 1.8g Fats: 18.9g Proteins: 18.7g Sodium: 464mg Sugar: 0.6g

Salmon Stew

Serves: 3
Prep Time: 20 mins

Ingredients
- 1 cup homemade fish broth
- 1 medium onion, chopped
- 1 pound salmon fillet, cubed
- Salt and black pepper, to taste
- 1 tablespoon butter

Directions
1) Season the salmon fillets with salt and black pepper.
2) Put butter and onions in a skillet and sauté for about 3 minutes.
3) Add salmon and cook for about 2 minutes on each side.
4) Stir in the fish broth and cover the lid.
5) Cook for about 7 minutes and dish out to serve hot.

Nutrition
Calories: 272 Carbs: 4.4g Fats: 14.2g Proteins: 32.1g Sodium: 275mg Sugar: 1.9g

Paprika Shrimp

Serves: 6
Prep Time: 25 mins

The paprika shrimp are a great summertime twist with good nutritional value.

Ingredients
- 6 tablespoons butter
- 1 teaspoon smoked paprika
- 2 pounds tiger shrimps
- Salt, to taste

Directions
1) Preheat the oven to 395 degrees F and grease a baking dish with butter.
2) Season the shrimps with smoked paprika and salt.
3) Arrange the seasoned shrimp in the baking dish and transfer the baking dish in oven.
4) Bake for about 15 minutes and dish out to serve.

Nutrition
Calories: 173 Carbs: 0.1g Fats: 8.3g Proteins: 23.8g Sodium: 332mg Sugar: 0g

Ketogenic Butter Fish

Serves: 3
Prep Time: 40 mins

The key here is getting the butter to a perfect, nutty brown, and it really does become another ingredient altogether.

Ingredients
- 2 tablespoons ginger-garlic paste
- 3 green chilies, chopped
- 1 pound salmon fillets
- Salt and black pepper, to taste
- ¾ cup butter

Directions
1) Season the salmon fillets with salt, black pepper, and ginger-garlic paste.
2) Place the salmon fillets in the pot and top with green chilies and butter.
3) Cover the lid and cook on LOW heat for about 30 minutes.
4) Dish out to serve hot.

Nutrition
Calories: 507 Carbs: 2.4g Fats: 45.9g Proteins: 22.8g Sodium: 296mg Sugar: 0.2g

Shrimp Magic

Serves: 3
Prep Time: 25 mins
Simple, fast, and delicious describes this Shrimp Magic recipe.

Ingredients
- 2 tablespoons butter
- ½ teaspoon smoked paprika
- 1 pound shrimps, peeled and deveined
- Lemongrass stalks
- 1 red chili pepper, seeded and chopped

Directions
1) Place all the ingredients in a bowl, except lemongrass, and mix well to marinate for about 2 hours.
2) Preheat the oven to 400 degrees F and thread the shrimps onto lemongrass stalks.
3) Bake for about 15 minutes and serve immediately.

Nutrition
Calories: 251 Carbs: 3g Fats: 10.3g Proteins: 34.6g Sodium: 424mg Sugar: 0.1g

Omega-Rich Dinner

Serves: 8
Prep Time: 40 mins

This Omega-Rich Dinner recipe is made using salmon fillets. Omega 3 nutrient is excellent for human health.

Ingredients
- 4 garlic cloves, minced
- Salt and black pepper, to taste
- 8 (6-ounce) skinless, boneless salmon fillets
- 2 tablespoons fresh lemon zest, grated finely
- 4 tablespoons olive oil
- 4 tablespoons fresh lemon juice

Directions
1) Preheat the grill to medium-high heat and grease the grill grate.
2) Put all the ingredients in a large bowl, except salmon fillets, and mix well.
3) Coat with garlic mixture generously and grill for about 7 minutes on each side.
4) Dish out to serve hot.

Nutrition
Calories: 278 Carbs: 1g Fats: 13.2g Proteins: 38.2g Sodium: 63mg Sugar: 0.3g

Sweet and Sour Fish

Serves: 3
Prep Time: 25 mins

Any kind of filleted fish can be substituted in this recipe.

Ingredients
- ¼ cup butter
- 2 drops liquid stevia
- 1 pound fish chunks
- Salt and black pepper, to taste
- 1 tablespoon vinegar

Directions
1) Heat butter in a large skillet and add fish chunks.
2) Cook for about 3 minutes and add liquid stevia and vinegar.
3) Cook for about 1 minute and add salt and black pepper.
4) Stir continuously at medium-low heat for about 10 minutes.
5) Place onto a serving bowl and serve hot.

Nutrition
Calories: 274 Carbs: 2.8g Fats: 15.4g Proteins: 33.2g Sodium: 604mg Sugar: 0g

Buttered Scallops

Serves: 6
Prep Time: 25 mins

A touch of butter makes this version of sea scallops special. This is also a great way to prepare fish fillets.

Ingredients
- 4 tablespoons fresh rosemary, chopped
- 4 garlic cloves, minced
- 2 pounds sea scallops
- Salt and black pepper, to taste
- ½ cup butter

Directions
1) Put butter, rosemary and garlic on medium-high heat and sauté for about 1 minute.
2) Stir in the sea scallops, salt, and black pepper and cook for about 2 minutes per side.
3) Add garlic and rosemary and sauté for about 3 minutes.
4) Dish out in a bowl and serve hot.

Nutrition
Calories: 279 Carbs: 5.7g Fats: 16.8g Proteins: 25.8g Sodium: 354mg Sugar: 0g

Buffalo Fish

Serves: 8
Prep Time: 20 mins

Salmon is a delicate fish that does well when lightly smoked and gently seasoned.

Ingredients
- Salt and black pepper, to taste
- 1 teaspoon garlic powder
- 3 tablespoons butter
- 1/3 cup Franks red hot sauce
- 3 salmon fillets

Directions
1) Put butter and fish fillets in a large skillet on medium heat.
2) Cook for about 2 minutes per side and add salt, garlic powder, and black pepper.
3) Cook for about 1 minute and add Franks red hot sauce.
4) Cover the lid and cook for about 7 minutes on low heat.
5) Dish out in a serving platter and serve hot.

Nutrition
Calories: 317 Carbs: 16.4g Fats: 22.7g Proteins: 13.6g Sodium: 659mg Sugar: 0.2g

BBQ Trout

Serves: 4
Prep Time: 20 mins

It is by far the best BBQ trout I have ever eaten. I like to serve it with roasted asparagus. Trout fish is highly advantageous to human health.

Ingredients
- 2 garlic cloves, crushed
- Salt and black pepper, to taste
- 4 rainbow trout fillets
- 1 small onion, sliced thinly
- 2 small lemons, seeded, sliced thinly and divided
- 1½ tablespoons olive oil

Directions
1) Preheat the grill to medium-high heat and grease the grill grate.
2) Rub the trout slices with garlic and arrange each trout slice over a piece of foil.
3) Arrange lemon and onion slices evenly over fillets and sprinkle with salt and black pepper.
4) Drizzle with olive oil and fold the foil pieces in order to seal the trout slices.
5) Grill the trout for about 6 minutes and serve hot.

Nutrition
Calories: 190 Carbs: 7g Fats: 13.4g Proteins: 13.5g Sodium: 361mg Sugar: 2.3g

Eggs and Dairy Recipes

Scrambled Eggs

Serves: 2
Prep Time: 15 mins

There is more to just mixing eggs and cooking! This is the right way to scramble eggs. It will make a believer out of you!

Ingredients
- 1 tablespoon butter
- Salt and black pepper, to taste
- 4 eggs, whisked
- 1 tablespoon milk

Directions
1) Combine together milk, eggs, salt, and black pepper in a medium bowl.
2) Put butter in a pan over medium-low heat and add the whisked eggs mixture slowly.
3) Stir continuously for about 4 minutes and dish onto a serving plate.

Nutrition
Calories: 151 Carbs: 0.7g Fats: 11.6g Proteins: 11.1g Sodium: 144mg Sugar: 0.7g

Pepperoni Omelet

Serves: 8
Prep Time: 15 mins

This is a family favorite for breakfast. Serve this along with sausage balls for a great brunch.

Ingredients
- 30 pepperoni slices
- 8 tablespoons cream
- 4 tablespoons butter
- 12 eggs
- Salt and freshly ground black pepper, to taste

Directions
1) Whisk together the eggs in a bowl and add the remaining ingredients.
2) Put butter in a pan and add the egg mixture.
3) Cook for about 2 minutes and flip the sides.
4) Cook for another 2 minutes and dish out in a serving plate.

Nutrition
Calories: 141 Carbs: 0.6g Fats: 11.3g Proteins: 8.9g Sodium: 334mg Sugar: 0.5g

Eggs Stuffed with Avocado and Watercress

Serves: 3
Prep Time: 15 mins

Greens are very good. Their taste is amazing. They have many benefits to human health.

Ingredients
- ½ medium ripe avocado, peeled, pitted and chopped
- ¼ tablespoon fresh lemon juice
- 3 organic eggs, boiled, peeled and cut in half lengthwise
- ¼ cup fresh watercress, trimmed
- Salt, to taste

Directions
1) Place a steamer basket at the bottom of the pot and pour water.
2) Put the watercress on the trivet and pour water in the pressure cooker.
3) Place the trivet in the cooker and lock the lid.
4) Cook for about 3 minutes at high pressure and then release the pressure quickly.
5) Drain the watercress completely and keep aside.
6) Remove the egg yolks and transfer into a bowl.
7) Mash watercress, lemon juice, avocado and salt completely with a fork.
8) Place the egg whites in a plate and stuff the egg whites with the watercress mixture.
9) Serve immediately.

Nutrition
Calories: 132 Carbs: 3.3g Fats: 10.9g Proteins: 6.3g Sodium: 65mg Sugar: 0.5g

Cheesy Mini Frittatas

Serves: 3
Prep Time: 25 mins

My family loves frittatas, and this is a quick and easy recipe for cheesy mini frittatas.

Ingredients

- 4 tablespoons cheddar cheese, shredded
- ¼ cup unsweetened almond milk
- 3 organic eggs
- 1 scallion, chopped
- ¼ teaspoon lemon pepper seasoning
- 2 cooked bacon slices, crumbled
- Salt and black pepper, to taste
- 1 medium zucchini, finely chopped

Directions

1) Preheat the oven to 400 degrees F and grease the silicone moulds.
2) Whisk together eggs and stir in the remaining ingredients, mixing well.
3) Pour the eggs mixture into the silicone moulds and transfer the moulds in the oven.
4) Bake for about 15 minutes and remove from the oven to serve.

Nutrition

Calories: 185 Carbs: 3.5g Fats: 13.2g Proteins: 13.6g Sodium: 435mg Sugar: 1.6g

Keto Coconut Pancakes

Serves: 4
Prep Time: 15 mins

This is a perfect breakfast preparation to break the monotony of eggs every day.

Ingredients
For Pancakes
- 4 eggs
- ¼ cup full-fat coconut milk
- ¼ cup melted ghee or grass-fed butter
- ½ tablespoon salt
- ½ tablespoon baking powder
- ¼ cup coconut flour

For Keto Caramel Sauce
- ¼ cup grass-fed butter
- ¼ cup full-fat coconut milk
- ½ tablespoon pure vanilla extract
- 1 pinch salt

Directions
For Pancakes
1) Take a non-stick skillet and heat butter or ghee in it at a low flame.
2) Now take a bowl and add butter, salt, milk, vanilla, and eggs to it.
3) Whisk and add coconut flour and baking powder. Keep whisking until a smooth mixture is formed.
4) Pour the batter to heated skillet and cook until the edges rise.
5) Flip and cook from the other side for a minute.
6) Add a bit of butter in between the batches to make the edges crispy.
7) Serve after topping with your favorite ones.

For Keto Caramel Sauce

1) Melt the butter in a small sauce pan until it turns brown and bubbly in appearance.
2) Add coconut milk and keep stirring until you achieve the thickness you desire.
3) Remove when it is boiled and add vanilla and salt to it.
4) Drizzle it over the pancakes to serve.
5) This sauce is in its best flavor, if used the same day.

Nutrition
Calories: 267 Carbs: 7.4g Fats: 24g Proteins: 7g Sodium: 943mg Sugar: 1.1g

Nut Porridge

Serves: 4
Prep Time: 25 mins

This hearty nut porridge is an energy packed, slow-release breakfast. You can also make it for a week.

Ingredients
- 4 teaspoons coconut oil, melted
- 1 cup pecan, halved
- 1 cup water
- 1 cup coconut milk
- 2 tablespoons stevia
- 1 cup cashew nuts, raw and unsalted

Directions
1) Place the cashew nuts and pecans in the food processor and pulse until chunked.
2) Put the chunked nuts into the pot and stir in coconut oil, stevia and water.
3) Cook for about 5 minutes on high heat and reduce the heat to low.
4) Simmer for about 10 minutes and dish out to serve.

Nutrition
Calories: 260 Carbs: 12.7g Fats: 22.9g Proteins: 5.6g Sodium: 9mg Sugar: 1.8g

Lemon Mousse

Serves: 4
Prep Time: 25 mins

A light and lovely mousse flavored with lemon! Serve it in tall stemmed glasses for an elegant finish.

Ingredients
- 1 cup heavy cream
- ¼ cup fresh lemon juice
- 1 teaspoon lemon liquid stevia
- 8-ounce cream cheese, softened
- ¼ teaspoon salt

Directions
1) Preheat the oven to 360 degrees F and grease 4 ramekins.
2) Mix together lemon liquid stevia, cream cheese, lemon juice, heavy cream, and salt in a bowl.
3) Pour the mixture into the ramekins and transfer the ramekins into the oven.
4) Bake for about 12 minutes and pour into the serving glasses.
5) Refrigerate for at least 2 hours and serve chilled.

Nutrition
Calories: 305 Carbs: 2.7g Fats: 31g Proteins: 5g Sodium: 299mg Sugar: 0.5g

Vanilla Yogurt

Serves: 12
Prep Time: 13 hours

A creamy and delicious yogurt with a subtle hint of vanilla!

Ingredients
- ½ tablespoon pure vanilla extract
- 2 scoops stevia
- ½ cup full-fat milk
- ¼ cup yogurt starter
- 1 cup heavy cream

Directions
1) Pour milk into the slow cooker and set it on low for about 2 hours.
2) Whisk vanilla extract, stevia and heavy cream in the slow cooker.
3) Allow the yogurt to sit and set the slow cooker on LOW to cook for about 3 hours.
4) Mix the yogurt starter with full-fat milk and return this mixture to the slow cooker.
5) Lock the lid of the slow cooker again and wrap it in two small towels.
6) Let the wrapped slow cooker to sit for about 8 hours and allow the yogurt to culture.
7) Dish out in a serving bowl or alternatively, store it by refrigerating.

Nutrition
Calories: 292 Carbs: 8.2g Fats: 26.2g Proteins: 5.2g Sodium: 86mg Sugar: 6.6g

Low Carb Blueberry Muffins

Serves: 6
Prep Time: 55 mins

A classic blueberry muffins recipe prepared for breakfast, keeping aligned your carb intake!

Ingredients

- 2 cups fresh blueberries
- 1 teaspoon cream of tartar
- ¼ cup coconut oil
- 4 eggs
- 1 pinch salt
- 1 teaspoon baking soda
- 1 teaspoon lemon juice
- 1/3 cup coconut flour
- 1 cup almonds, ground
- ½ cup coconut yogurt

Directions

1) Separate eggs yolks and heat oven to 350 degrees F.
2) Take a bowl and mix lemon juice, coconut oil, and egg yolks.
3) Add baking soda, ground almonds, flax seeds, salt, coconut flour, and coconut yogurt to it and mix.
4) Use an electric egg beater to beat egg whites and add tartar cream after 30 seconds.
5) Fold egg whites into dough first and then add blueberries.
6) Line a non-stick muffin tray and grease it with coconut oil.
7) Bake in an oven for 30-35 minutes. Remove from heat and cool for 10 minutes before removing tins.
8) Muffins can be frozen for two months and kept at room temperature for four days.

Nutrition

Calories: 278 Carbs: 16.7g Fats: 21.1g Proteins: 8.8g Sodium: 280mg Sugar: 6.9g

Keto Quiche

Serves: 8
Prep Time: 25 mins

A perfect breakfast recipe to lighten you up for a bright day! It gives you abundant fats to utilize as body fuel.

Ingredients
- 8 large eggs
- ¼ cup greens
- ¼ cup onions
- ¼ pound bacon
- ½ tablespoon salt
- 1 cup full-fat coconut milk
- 1 cup nut flour
- ¼ cup nutritional yeast
- ¼ cup coconut oil

Directions
1) Heat oven up to 400°F and grease an 8" pan lightly.
2) Mix the flour with coconut oil, eggs, and salt to form dough.
3) Press this dough into spring form pan in a way that the crust rises to the sides. Then poke holes with a fork.
4) Place spring form pan on a sheet pan to allow baking for 10 minutes.
5) Add bacons or greens according to your desire.
6) Bake for 30-40 minutes at a temp of 350 degrees F.
7) Slice when cooled.

Nutrition
Calories: 347 Carbs: 13.8g Fats: 27.5g Proteins: 15.4g Sodium: 847mg Sugar: 5.6g

Vegetarian Recipes

Tofu with Mushrooms

Serves: 6
Prep Time: 30 mins

Versatile and easy to cook with, tofu takes on many roles and adapts well to the flavors of marinades and sauces.

Ingredients
- 2 cups fresh mushrooms, chopped finely
- 8 tablespoons Parmesan cheese, shredded
- 2 blocks tofu, pressed and cubed into 1-inch pieces
- 8 tablespoons butter
- Salt and freshly ground black pepper, to taste

Directions
1) Mix together tofu, salt and black pepper in a bowl.
2) Put butter and seasoned tofu in a pan over medium-low heat.
3) Cook for about 5 minutes and stir in the mushrooms and Parmesan cheese.
4) Cook for about 4 minutes, occasionally stirring and dish onto a serving plate.

Nutrition
Calories: 211 Carbs: 2g Fats: 18.5g Proteins: 11.5g Sodium: 346mg Sugar: 0.5g

Bacon Veggies Combo

Serves: 4
Prep Time: 35 mins

This recipe is considered as a good breakfast. It uses garlic, which has many benefits to health, one of which is that it controls blood pressure.

Ingredients
- 1 green bell pepper, seeded and chopped
- 2 scallions, chopped
- 4 bacon slices
- 3 garlic cloves, minced
- ½ cup Parmesan Cheese
- 1 tablespoon avocado mayonnaise

Directions
1) Preheat the oven to 380 degrees F and grease a baking dish.
2) Arrange the bacon slices in the baking dish and top with scallions, bell peppers, avocado mayonnaise, and Parmesan Cheese.
3) Bake for about 25 minutes and serve immediately.

Nutrition
Calories: 197 Carbs: 4.7g Fats: 13.8g Proteins: 14.3g Sodium: 662mg Sugar: 1.9g

Onion Tofu Scramble

Serves: 4
Prep Time: 20 mins

This recipe is a perfect combination of onions and tofu. It is best for the vegetarian people who want to follow a ketogenic diet.

Ingredients
- 4 tablespoons butter
- 2 blocks tofu, pressed and cubed into 1 inch pieces
- 1 cup cheddar cheese, grated
- Salt and black pepper, to taste
- 2 medium onions, sliced

Directions
1) Season tofu with salt and black pepper in a bowl.
2) Put butter and onions in a pan over medium-low heat.
3) Cook for about 3 minutes and add tofu mixture.
4) Cook for about 2 minutes and add cheddar cheese.
5) Cover with lid and cook for about 5 minutes on low heat.
6) Dish in a bowl to serve for breakfast.

Nutrition
Calories: 184 Carbs: 6.3g Fats: 7.3g Proteins: 12.2g Sodium: 222mg Sugar: 2.7g

Ham Spinach Blast

Serves: 4
Prep Time: 40 mins

The taste of ham and spinach combination is amazing. Spinach has many benefits to human health.

Ingredients

- ¼ cup cream
- Salt and black pepper, to taste
- 1½ pounds fresh baby spinach
- 14-ounce ham, sliced
- 2 tablespoons butter, melted

Directions

1) Preheat the oven to 375 degrees F and grease 4 ramekins with butter.
2) Put butter and spinach in a pan over medium-low heat.
3) Cook for about 3 minutes and drain the liquid from the spinach completely.
4) Return spinach in the pan and top with ham slices, cream, salt, and black pepper.
5) Bake for about 25 minutes and dish into a large serving bowl to serve hot.

Nutrition

Calories: 188 Carbs: 4.9g Fats: 12.5g Proteins: 14.6g Sodium: 1098mg Sugar: 0.3g

Bacon Bok Choy Samba

Serves: 6
Prep Time: 25 mins

Bacon and bok choy are used in this recipe, making this samba a perfect breakfast dance in your mouth!

Ingredients
- 2 tablespoons olive oil
- 4 bacon slices
- 8 tablespoons cream
- 8 bok choy, sliced
- Salt and black pepper, to taste
- 1 cup Parmesan cheese, grated

Directions
1) Season bok choy with salt and black pepper.
2) Put olive oil and bacon slices in a skillet on medium-high heat.
3) Sauté for about 5 minutes and stir in cream and bok choy.
4) Sauté for about 6 minutes and sprinkle with Parmesan cheese.
5) Cook for about 4 minutes on low heat and dish out in a serving platter.

Nutrition
Calories: 112 Carbs: 1.9g Fats: 4.9g Proteins: 3g Sodium: 355mg Sugar: 0.8g

Garlic Parmesan Fried Eggplant

Serves: 12
Prep Time: 30 mins

These fried eggplant slices are certain to please when dipped in a mixture of garlic, almond flour, and parmesan cheese.

Ingredients
- 1 teaspoon salt
- 2 medium eggplants, cut into 1/3 inch thick slices
- 2 large eggs
- 2 cups almond flour
- 4 teaspoons garlic powder
- 1 teaspoon black pepper
- 2 cups Parmesan cheese grated
- 1 teaspoon salt
- ½ cup butter

Directions
1) Arrange the eggplants in a single layer in a dish and season with salt.
2) Whisk together eggs in a shallow bowl.
3) Mix together Parmesan, almond flour, garlic powder, salt, and black pepper in another bowl.
4) Heat butter in a large skillet over medium heat.
5) Dip each slice of eggplant in egg and then coat with almond flour mixture.
6) Drop the eggplant slices in a skillet in batches and fry until browned.
7) Dish out and serve with your favorite dip.

Nutrition
Calories: 271 Carbs: 10g Fats: 22g Proteins: 12g Sodium: 696mg Sugar: 2.6g

Roasted Broccoli and Cauliflower

Serves: 6
Prep Time: 25 mins

I made this recipe for my family for the first time, and they went back for seconds!

Ingredients
- 1 cup Parmesan cheese, grated
- 2 cups broccoli florets
- 2 cups cauliflower florets
- Salt and black pepper, to taste
- ½ cup butter

Directions
1) Preheat the oven to 395 degrees F and grease a baking dish.
2) Mix the butter, cauliflower florets, broccoli florets, salt, and black pepper in a bowl.
3) Transfer to baking dish and top with Parmesan cheese.
4) Place the baking dish in the oven and bake for about 15 minutes.
5) Remove from the oven to serve hot.

Nutrition
Calories: 169 Carbs: 4g Fats: 16.5g Proteins: 3.2g Sodium: 172mg Sugar: 1.3g

Creamed Peas

Serves: 3
Prep Time: 25 mins
This is a quick and easy way to make this side dish for 3 people without all the fuss.

Ingredients
- 1 cup frozen green peas, thawed
- 1 cup water
- Salt, to taste
- 1 cup heavy cream
- 3 tablespoons butter

Directions
1) Put the butter and frozen peas in the pot and sauté for about 2 minutes.
2) Add salt, heavy cream, and water and cover the lid.
3) Cook for about 10 minutes on medium-low heat and dish out to serve hot.

Nutrition
Calories: 279 Carbs: 8.1g Fats: 26.5g Proteins: 3.6g Sodium: 152mg Sugar: 2.8g

Whole Garlic Roast

Serves: 4
Prep Time: 25 mins

You can peel off a clove of the garlic and literally squeeze the garlic from its shell onto the bread or cracker.

Ingredients
- 4 tablespoons herbed butter
- 1 cup water
- Salt and black pepper, to taste
- 4 large garlic bulbs

Directions
1) Preheat the oven to 395 degrees F and grease a baking dish.
2) Season the garlic bulbs with salt and pepper.
3) Transfer in the baking dish and top with herbed butter.
4) Place the baking dish in the oven and bake for about 15 minutes.
5) Remove from the oven and serve hot.

Nutrition
Calories: 117 Carbs: 3g Fats: 11.5g Proteins: 0.1g Sodium: 84mg Sugar: 0g

Grilled Halloumi Salad

Serves: 6
Prep Time: 15 mins

Give halloumi a try in your next salad for some added fat and protein if you are a vegetarian and sticking to a low carb/keto diet.

Ingredients
- 3 cucumbers, sliced
- 1½ oz walnuts, chopped
- 9 oz halloumi cheese, cut into 1/3 inch slices
- 3 handful baby arugula
- Olive oil
- Salt, to taste
- Balsamic vinegar

Directions
1) Grill the halloumi cheese for about 5 minutes per side to achieve grill marks on both sides.
2) Put cucumbers, walnuts and arugula in a bowl and place halloumi cheese on the top.
3) Sprinkle some salt and top with balsamic vinegar and olive oil to serve.

Nutrition
Calories: 259 Carbs: 9.8g Fats: 19.9g Proteins: 13.4g Sodium: 269mg Sugar: 3.7g

Snacks and Appetizers Recipes

Spinach Quiche

Serves: 6
Prep Time: 45 mins

I don't normally like cooked spinach, but I fell in love with this at first bite because it's so heavenly!

Ingredients
- 1 tablespoon butter, melted
- Salt and black pepper, to taste
- 1 (10-ounce) package frozen spinach, thawed
- 5 organic eggs, beaten
- 3 cups Monterey Jack cheese, shredded

Directions
1) Preheat the oven to 360 degrees F and grease a 9-inch pie dish lightly.
2) Put butter and spinach in a large skillet on medium-low heat.
3) Cook for about 3 minutes and set aside.
4) Mix together Monterey Jack cheese, spinach, eggs, salt, and black pepper in a bowl.
5) Put the mixture into prepared pie dish and transfer into the oven.
6) Bake for about 30 minutes and remove from the oven.
7) Cut into equal sized wedges and serve hot.

Nutrition
Calories: 349 Carbs: 3.2g Fats: 27.8g Proteins: 23g Sodium: 532mg Sugar: 1.3g

Cheese Casserole

Serves: 6
Prep Time: 40 mins

This recipe is very forgiving, so you can add or remove ingredients, according to your taste!

Ingredients
- 10 ounce parmesan, shredded
- 16 ounce marinara sauce
- 2 tablespoons olive oil
- 2 pounds sausage scramble
- 16 ounce mozzarella cheese, shredded

Directions
1) Preheat the oven to 395 degrees F and grease olive oil on the baking dish.
2) Arrange half of the sausage scramble in the baking dish and layer with half of the marinara sauce.
3) Top with half of the mozzarella and Parmesan cheese.
4) Layer with the remaining half of the sausage scramble and spread the remaining half of Parmesan and mozzarella cheese.
5) Top with rest of the marinara sauce and bake in the oven for about 25 minutes.
6) Dish onto a casserole and serve hot.

Nutrition
Calories: 521 Carbs: 6g Fats: 38.8g Proteins: 35.4g Sodium: 201mg Sugar: 5.4g

Mixed Nuts

Serves: 16
Prep Time: 25 mins

The foods in this easy recipe are a powerhouse of nutrition, providing high antioxidants and fiber from nuts.

Ingredients
- 1 cup raw peanuts
- Salt, to taste
- 1 cup raw almonds
- 1 tablespoon butter, melted
- ½ cup raw cashew nuts

Directions
1) Preheat the oven at 330 degrees F and grease a baking dish.
2) Put the peanuts, almonds and cashew nuts in a baking dish and transfer into the oven.
3) Bake for about 12 minutes, tossing twice in between.
4) Dish out the nuts from the oven into a bowl and add salt and melted butter.
5) Toss to coat well and return the nuts mixture to the oven.
6) Bake for about 5 more minutes and dish out to serve.

Nutrition
Calories: 189 Carbs: 6.6g Fats: 16.5g Proteins: 6.8g Sodium: 19mg Sugar: 1.3g

Broccoli Pops

Serves: 6
Prep Time: 20 mins

This is a great recipe that is really easy to make. Plus, you don't have to worry about your waist line!

Ingredients

- 1/3 cup Parmesan cheese, grated
- 2 cups cheddar cheese, grated
- Salt and black pepper, to taste
- 3 eggs, beaten
- 3 cups broccoli florets
- 1 tablespoon olive oil

Directions

1) Preheat the oven to 360 degrees F and grease a baking dish with olive oil.
2) Pulse the broccoli in a food processor until finely crumbed.
3) Add broccoli and stir in rest of the ingredients in a large bowl.
4) Make small equal-sized balls from the mixture.
5) Put the balls in a baking sheet and refrigerate for at least 30 minutes.
6) Place balls in the baking dish and transfer the dish into the oven.
7) Bake for about 13 minutes and dish out to serve.

Nutrition

Calories: 162 Carbs: 1.9g Fats: 12.4g Proteins: 11.2g Sodium: 263mg Sugar: 0.5g

Keto Onion Rings

Serves: 4
Prep Time: 20 mins

This is a great snack during the day or clever contribution to a holiday party.

Ingredients
- 2 large onions, cut into ¼ inch slices
- 2 teaspoons baking powder
- Salt, to taste
- 2 cups cream cheese
- 2 eggs

Directions
1) Preheat the oven to 375 degrees F and separate the onion slices into rings.
2) Mix together salt and baking powder in a bowl.
3) Whisk together cream cheese and eggs in another dish.
4) Dredge the onion rings into baking powder mixture and dip into cream cheese mixture.
5) Place the onion rings in the oven and bake for about 10 minutes.
6) Dish out to serve hot.

Nutrition
Calories: 266 Carbs: 9.9g Fats: 22.5g Proteins: 8g Sodium: 285mg Sugar: 3.5g

Mexican Inspired Beef Soup

Serves: 12
Prep Time: 20 mins

This is a quick, throw together soup with a Mexican flair. Teenagers love it!

Ingredients
- 1 pound grass-fed lean ground beef
- 2 cups homemade beef broth
- 1 tablespoon chili powder
- ¼ cup cheddar cheese, shredded
- 10-ounce canned sugar-free diced tomatoes with green chiles
- 2 garlic cloves, minced
- 4-ounce cream cheese
- Salt and black pepper, to taste
- ½ teaspoon olive oil
- ¼ cup heavy cream
- 1 teaspoon ground cumin

Directions
1) Place the oil and beef in the pressure cooker and sauté for about 8 minutes.
2) Stir in the remaining ingredients, except cheddar cheese, and cover the lid.
3) Cook at high pressure for about 10 minutes and do the natural pressure release.
4) Top with cheddar cheese and serve hot.

Nutrition
Calories: 405 Carbs: 6.7g Fats: 26.7g Proteins: 31.1g Sodium: 815mg Sugar: 3.5g

Zucchini Cream Cheese Fries

Serves: 4
Prep Time: 20 mins

This is a quick and easy recipe that tastes delicious. Try this recipe as a tasty summer or spring side dish.

Ingredients
- 1 cup cream cheese
- 1 pound zucchini, sliced into 2 ½-inch sticks
- 2 tablespoons olive oil
- Salt, to taste

Directions
1) Preheat the oven to 380 degrees F and grease a baking dish with olive oil.
2) Season the zucchini with salt and coat with cream cheese.
3) Place zucchini in the baking dish and transfer into the oven.
4) Bake for about 10 minutes and dish out to serve.

Nutrition
Calories: 374 Carbs: 7.1g Fats: 36.6g Proteins: 7.7g Sodium: 294mg Sugar: 2.8g

Asparagus Bites

Serves: 6
Prep Time: 20 mins

This recipe is perfect for people who are on a keto diet and love asparagus.

Ingredients
- 1 cup desiccated coconut
- 2 cups asparagus
- 1 cup feta cheese

Directions
1) Preheat the oven to 400 degrees F and grease a baking dish with cooking spray.
2) Place the desiccated coconut in a shallow dish and coat asparagus evenly with coconut.
3) Arrange the coated asparagus in the baking dish and top with cheese.
4) Transfer into the oven and bake for about 10 minutes to serve.

Nutrition
Calories: 135 Carbs: 5g Fats: 10.3g Proteins: 7g Sodium: 421mg Sugar: 3.1g

Scallion Cake

Serves: 4
Prep Time: 30 mins

This recipe is very good for people who are on a low carb diet as it helps in weight loss.

Ingredients
- ¼ cup flax seeds meal
- ½ cup Parmesan cheese, grated finely
- ½ teaspoon baking powder
- ½ cup low-fat cottage cheese
- 1/3 cup scallion, sliced thinly
- ½ cup almond meal
- ¼ cup nutritional yeast flakes
- 6 organic eggs, beaten
- ½ cup raw hemp seeds
- Salt, to taste

Directions
1) Preheat the oven to 390 degrees F and grease 4 ramekins with oil.
2) Mix together salt, baking powder, almond meal, hemp seeds and flax seeds meal in a large bowl.
3) Mix cottage cheese and eggs in another bowl and transfer this mixture into almond meal mixture.
4) Mix until well combined and gently add scallions.
5) Transfer the mixture evenly into ramekins and bake for about 20 minutes.
6) Remove from the oven and serve warm.

Nutrition
Calories: 306 Carbs: 10.7g Fats: 19.7g Proteins: 23.5g Sodium: 398mg Sugar: 1.3g

Avocado Chips

Serves: 2
Prep Time: 20 mins

If you are craving snacks, you can make it in just 20 minutes!

Ingredients
- 2 raw avocados, peeled and sliced in chips form
- 2 tablespoons butter
- Salt and freshly ground pepper, to taste

Directions
1) Preheat the oven to 365 degrees F and grease a baking dish.
2) Top with butter and avocado slices and transfer into the oven.
3) Bake for about 10 minutes and season with salt and black pepper to serve.

Nutrition
Calories: 391 Carbs: 15g Fats: 38.2g Proteins: 3.5g Sodium: 96mg Sugar: 0.5g

Conclusion

During the process of ketosis, the body changes its energy source from glucose to fat. When you switch to the keto diet, your body initially tends to consume your inner body fat for its overall functioning, logically explaining how effective it is in lowering your weight. As soon as the insulin content in your body is lowered, fat loss is improved, and you lose weight without getting hungry.

The keto diet plan is very effective, not only in drastic weight and fat loss but also offering a number of healthy benefits ranging from reversing type-2 diabetes to preventing serious health conditions like cancer. The effect of the keto diet plan might vary from person to person and isn't solely related to drastic weight loss. It is a lifestyle, not merely a quick way to lose weight only. Kick start your keto today!

Made in the USA
Middletown, DE
12 April 2019